CELTO-PHILIA

Poems in English
USING
Traditional Celtic Forms
(plus a few just on Celtic themes)

b y

Gary Kent Spain

Poet-Fiddler
(and discoverer of the lost core
of the Kabbalah)

may

Lugh

smile

on this venture

Happy Harp
[Óglachas of Rannaigheacht Bheag]

Happy travail: carve candy
for ear's stale, starving pantry
with terse wit, to form fancy
verse fit to make *harp* happy.

***Prose-Poetry*, the Oxymoron**
[Cyhydedd Naw Ban (starts with Cyhydedd Hir)]

Gather round, o ye
deprived progeny
of Modernity,
      the religion.
News flash. Nothing new has arisen
to rock the fundamental mission
of poet: to speak crisp precision
on multi-levels, like a griffon.
That is the crux: magic! to listen
with two heads, multi-mirrored (bidden).
Prose is not like that. Prose sticks one tongue
only into the mix of what's sung:
it infiltrates not, but is just flung.
Keep lines pure: mix not prose thereamong.
How else might praise reach the highest rung!
How else might those on guard still get stung!
They're like oil and water, fit perhaps
to mark sinkings or other mishaps,
but to soar, I implore: wear your chaps,
for the swift steed of fewer words waits
only to be called forth by your aches.

Preface

As poet I have delved into the forest of medieval Welsh *cynghanedd* (missing from the above) and cross-rhymes of Irish *Dán Díreach* far more, surely, than any other poet composing in English. (Welsh poets may find my interpretation of cynghanedd inexact with regard to half-lines and caesuras, to which I can only plead the extreme difficulty of its use in English.) I try virtually every form I come across, to add to my stable of verbal horses, and Celtic measures hold a special attraction for me, for three reasons.

One, the *bethluisnion* tree alphabet, preserved in Irish lore, is the one indispensible key to the lost core of teachings that underlie the Jewish Kabbalah, whose tradition concerning letters is demonstrably akin to that of the Celts. Robert Graves, in *The White Goddess*, makes it clear, as does a passage in the (controversial) *Barddas* of Iolo Morganwg, that the tradition linking letters to numbers was preserved also in Wales. I have penned a book explaining what you end up with when you put the Celtic lore together with what has survived of Kabbalah: having decayed each by a different route, the two branches *fill each other's holes* to reveal an original trunk that is an awesome concentration of knowledge, including of chemistry, particle physics, and metaphysics, knowledge most likely handed down from the last civilization—destroyed by meltings at the end of the last ice age? The book is *World Egg in the Cauldron of Art: The Restored Lost Core of Kabbalah and Its Scientific Implications*.

Two, I am fascinated by the lore of dark ages Britain, especially that surrounding Taliesin and the two Merlins, or Myrddins, listed in the Welsh *Triads* as Britain's foremost 'baptismal' bards. I feel all three may have had a hand in preserving bardic lore in Britain so that a modern such as myself *could* put it together with Judaic tradition to reveal wonders. The connection here with my first reason (above) includes the name *Taliesin* itself, which meant 'Radiant Brow' and may have been more title than name, bestowed after a rebirth (i.e. initiation) on someone *named* Gwion; for it calls to mind the Lurianic Kabbalah's teaching about *Adam Qadmon*—'Primordial Man'—and the rays emanating from His forehead. On another tack, Nennius, the earliest extant British history (after Gildas, who was no historian), makes no distinction between the Ambrosius who was child prodigy Merlin and him who was the great military leader Ambrosius Aurelianus. So I dispute the modern claim that the name *Merlin* was just an attempt to euphemize *Myrddin* because of its supposed similarity to a French crudity: it is clear to me from Celts' tendency to confuse M and V that AVRELIANUS must have evolved from AMRELIANUS to MERLINUS (accent on penultimate syllable). This was the first 'Merlin'; the second, who lived a century later, was Myrddin ap Morvryn, or Myrddin Wyllt, also called Lailoken, from Welsh *Llallawg*, 'twin brother' (meaning of Gwyneth, wife of Rhydderch Hael of Strathclyde).

And three, the considerable difficulty of the Celtic measures and their prescribed manner of embellishment constituted a challenge to my ability at rhyming and consonance, thus offering an opportunity to improve my skill. I also became interested in the sixth-century verse structure and sound figures revealed in *The Gododdin of Aneirin: Text and Context from Dark-Age North Britain*, edited by John T. Koch, who reconstructed the *Gododdin*'s original Brittonic text. This old style of verse attracts me for its *freedom*—much like Germanic strong-stress alliterative verse (what I, descended from Vikings, call 'rowing meter')—in that the syllable count is allowed to vary, though oddly enough carefully avoiding 13-syllable lines (a custom I too follow).

I have mixed feelings about Welsh *cynghanedd*: on the one hand, it is a challenge and can be musically rich; on the other hand, according to Graves it was once used as status symbol for excluding from court those minstrels who preserved the older strata of myth and legend that eventually became the romances. Let me make it clear: I am no court bard, either by status or inclination, for I am much too rebellious (and of the 'minstrel' class). But I *am* drawn to the music of cynghanedd.

I originally sought out Celtic measures in search of some technique beyond mere metrical rhymed verse in terms of form, but found they utilized rhyme to an even greater degree. Yet the *way* they used it—cross-rhymes in Irish, internal rhyme and repetition of consonant sequences in Welsh—draws ear's attention *away* from the end-rhyme and so actually does accomplish what I originally sought, albeit in an entirely unexpected way! It is a little like the use of counterpoint in Baroque music—disappearance of which in the Classical era made *its* imprisoned structures sound like endless reams of rhymed metrical verse without letup (hence my dream of starting a *Classical-free* classical music station). The effect of counterpoint is like a three-ring circus: if what is happening in one ring grows dull, what is occurring in another will draw the attention.

Speaking of music, my other skill (I only have two) is a well developed musical ear. I play Irish airs and jigs (and the occasional reel, though there I am no whiz) on fiddle and have written a hundred or more songs on the guitar. I grew up studying classical violin. My father (Delbert Spain, amateur actor and Shakespeare aficionado), who raised me on the Bard's plays, discussed poetic rhythm with me at length when he was writing his book *Shakespeare Sounded Soundly: The Verse Structure and the Language*. For he suspected my musical training might yield insights on the subject of rhythm that he lacked. It was my mother from whom I inherited my musical genes; she played all sorts of instruments, including pedal organ; my dad, poor guy, was tone deaf (meaning he lacked any sense of pitch). I consider my choice of parents this time round exceptionally fortuitous. Still, neither skill has been very remunerative, though I confess I had an opportunity to make decent money as a computer programmer (following in my father's footsteps) but gave it up after a few years as I found I could not continue at it and remain a poet of any consequence: the two skills appeared to fight over the same region of my brain.

I only began discovering specifics of Celtic versification around 2010, so poems herein are mostly a product of the last dozen-plus years—the work of my dotage (I am just an old hippy whom destiny left loitering about in the aftermath). Let us proceed, then, without further ado.

GKSpain
28 Oct 2023

Table of Contents

Cywydd Deuair Hirion

Cyhydedd Fer

Byr a Thoddaid

Clogyrnach

Cywydd Llosgyrnog

Rhupunt

Measures Allowed the Chief Bard

The Dark Ages

Mixtures of Forms

For Love of the Gaels   79

Rannaigheacht Bheag

Rannaigheacht Ghairid

Rannaigheacht Mhor

Deibhidhe

Séadna

Droighneach (Modern Specs)

Droighneach (Old School)

Miscellaneous Irish Forms

Celtic-Themed Poems in Other Forms

APPENDIX: *Moral and Metaphysical Themes* 139

Total: 233

CELTOPHILIA

For Love of the Britons

English-Language Poet Utilizes Welsh and Proto-Welsh Measures

(Poems conforming to specifications of cynghanedd *have [(c)] after the title.)*

The Contents of Urns
[Cyhydedd Naw Ban]

There is a subtle pull to awen,
that driving flow of inspiration
ending up lines. Become the question
and answer draws you to its bosom.
Trust the phrases' burgeoning rhythm
the subconscious spews from soul's chasm
and build on its hybrid momentum,
that mixture made of aim plus patterns
available to the ear—what yearns
to manifest in the verbal ferns
each green mind honoring the Muse earns
as wages for the sin of nocturnes
and antic airs airing in tall urns.

The Englyn

The *englyn* is meant to stand alone as a succinct statement—a bit like haiku? But I approached the measure *Englyn Penfyr* early on as if it were a stanza to be used in longer poems. I have reworked some of this so that each *englyn* can at least stand on its own as a statement. These are followed by a few in off-beat *englyn* forms, then *Englyn Milwr,* a form of which I am inordinately fond (for its simplicity).

Bardic Instruction Tape

Intro

Be not as most moderns tow'rds sounds; for speech
can reach beyond mundane bounds,
beyond the jaws of hell-hounds.

Sounds *boom!* and sounds *drive the wind!* and sounds *hiss!*
sounds' kiss is how poets bend
hearts to causes, how hearts mend.

Song can soar, whether in praise, or to cry,
or a barb let fly that flays
a chief's soul cheap in his ways.

Learn your letters, known long past; sounds that serve
to unnerve, or soothe: they cast
each a spell whose roar holds fast.

For ears' gift shall I recite, in spare terms,
what one learns, through rays of Light,
from druids' vast inner might.

Consonant-Months[*]

Beth is for *birch*, the sun's birth: yuletide's call
to all, a mere infant's worth
rising anew from the earth.

Luis is learning's sheltered young: *rowan*'s boon
that soon pays dividends sprung
from our lucidness of tongue.

Nion means *not* to have, hence need: *ash*, the wood
of good tool handles, man's steed
for things newly made by deed.

Fearn, flutes' *alder*, is Bran's tree: start of spring,
head singing to shield the free—
this boar I wear around me.

Saille[†] or *sallow*, growth's gush, pollen's spray,
willow's woven way of lush
spring's incipient new rush.

Straif, *blackthorn*, strife, La Mère du Bois, vanguard
of wood's hard fight come spring thaw
to retake fields from crows' caw.

Huath, *hawthorn*'s hedge, its buds white, purified:
its thorns divide, like space (night
from day's sensual delight).

Duir as in *dur*mast, stout door, *oak* spread wide
that bolts might ride it and roar:
summer's start; what looms before.

---

[*] Tree-names not footnoted (other than *ura* and *ixias*) are single-syllable.
[†] (pronounced "SAL-yuh")

Tinne[*], tav, one's mark, one's word: *holly* pricks
if it sticks close, like a herd
(since one leaf's prick is absurd).

Coll concentrates wisdom's force, *hazel*'s truth—
age, not youth—in thinking's course:
inspired insight, gaunt remorse.

Quert the *apple* is asking's fruit: man's quest,
Myrddin's nest against pursuit
(English *whuh* with the *q* mute).

Muin's *mm* greets the ripened *vine*, in the sun,
late summer done: harvest time,
start of fall, of love, of wine.

Gort must get, to give: desire—to climb walls,
ivy crawls across the mire
that to heights it might aspire.

nGetal[†] engages healing's arts: *reed* thatch,
or plastered patch where wound smarts,
straw that herbs to throat imparts.

Peith, whose prophecies abide, leaves its trace
in **nGetal**'s place: ink from dried
whitten berries spread words wide.

Ruis, 'red', from the beads *elder* bears: it rues
clues that at its death it stares,
wood that burns with devils' airs.

Vowel-Seasons

Ailm[‡] awes by height: yuletide *fir*, or *pines*
in Shakespeare's lines, what will stir
our *ah*s when new moons occur.

---

[*] (pronounced "TIN-yuh")
[†] (pronounced "NYEH-dl")
[‡] (pronounced "AH-luv")

Onn opens spring's blossoms—*oh!*—hence the *furze*
whose yellow stirs growth's onflow,
color that makes the moon grow.

Ura oozes with summer's sap: soft *heath*
beneath star-met lovers' 'nap'
with the full moon in their lap.

Ailm echoes fir with *palm*: a warm place
in *space*, not time, boon of calm,
rest from life's pace, reward's balm.

Eadhe[*] is aging autumn's "eh?" *aspen*,
whose leaves blazon breezes' sway:
moon past full, waning away.

Idho[†] ekes out aeons' cold, winter's due,
the *yew*, ending up an old
moon caught fleeing from the fold.

Ixias in Greek, Yule's *y*, *mistletoe*,
poised to grow only on high:
tree-nester, moon's dark goodbye.

End-Remarks

These were lessons druids knew and instilled
in their skilled bards, fortune's few,
tasked with words that stir man's stew.

Man's contract with nature's law? Words that ring
with truth's sting past tongue and jaw
and tooth: mind's hymn to its awe.

---

[*] (pronounced "EH-yuh")
[†] (pronounced "EE-yoh" or perhaps "EE-yodh")

Song of the Wolf

You hound us, man, because we share your taste,
will eat in haste what you, there,
might hoard, because we wolves dare.

We ignore fixed boundaries you impose,
borders you chose just to please
a life centered around ease.

You stay in place most of your year, while we
run free, seeking the wild deer
or lesser game without fear.

We dread no creature but you, whom we grant
your space, since scant game wends through
lands that have seen what you do.

Herds you keep, though, attract our paws, since game
is all the same, luring jaws
of those that know not man's laws.

But know this, man: we do not seek *your* flesh
to enmesh in teeth, for meek
though your young be, you all reek.

You smell of predator, not prey, and we
have learned to flee your warm way
of guns and wolf-traps that say:

"You may not share with us this earth, our home,
which you roam: when pressed by dearth
of game, give man a wide berth!"

With the Ocean's Eyes [*(c)*]
[*Englyn Unodl Union*]

"I am no longer just one drop / I have become the entire sea." Rumi

Ought see with means to soothe the mess—truth's reach,
not wrath's rut—to buttress
a kind outlook and dent less,
caress more, our core sameness.

Planet Neptune [*(c)*]
[*Englyn Unodl Crwca*]

Air's channel for stars' chill fire
to light wooed seas' tilted shire,
ringed as if a wrong desire—shadow-drawn
on the mat of satire.

Some Trees Work Too Hard [*(c)*]
[*Englyn Proest Gadwynog*]

What we will give who tell gain
appear! draw near! Add renown
and no room need now remain
for moonlight in her nightgown.

Bless Us, the Imperfect [*(c)*]
[*Englyn Proest Dalgron*]

I can't *not* be content: been
aloft on down-soft wind. Sun,
run among us, warming on;
tease us for one more season.

Five 'Soldier's Englyns'

Poetry

Forum where words warm others,
verse born of swarms of mothers,
your crisp form's shorn what smothers.

A Jab at King Jabber (Obama)

Promise no vice, though it be;
compromise not: advice-free,
you *improvise* misery!

Far-Off Love

Treat well the ones you soften
and think on me not often
but well, o pool I quaff in.

Self-Satire

He strives mightily for grounds
in insight to mine for mounds
of gripes using tight-wound sounds.

The Lot

Though some fail to flay the theme,
all the lot are what they seem
in gleeman's eye (aye, a gleam).

Ode to Honor [*(c)*]

Mask, redesign my scarred zen,
warmed in still's broth: 'twill soften
once shown there moan other men.

See crowed battle scoured by toll
clean of fruit: come the drum-roll,
who remain then gain the goal.

Love's Game [*(c)*]
[repeated consonants in tree-calendar order with St (Ss) displaced to the end]

Belie no face: blown, if seen.
Hide to calk, who'd take a queen.
Mug pierced past my gap pristine.

Hyperborean Apollo

Sun sways to the unremarked
drumbeat on which earth's embarked,
on whose skin all skill is parked.

Tall priests of Apollo taught
wisdom the North Wind had brought,
lack of which rates next to naught—

Britons flowered, with the mists
of now not yet formed, those twists
and turns masking what exists.

Behind Boreas, gusts blew
trumpets; harps were plucked by dew
gathering the old anew.

Awdl Gywydd

Conveying the simple beauty of what the Irish call *aicill* rhyme.

Cunedda in Gwynedd [*(c)*]

Reviled, exiled, he gazes
at places new to pillage.
Foes Britons' talons too long
let wrong them still steal tillage.

With blows forced, the bile is first
to flow, immersed: innate flame
past and yet to be, fleeing
defeat's sting, din new fights tame.

To high fray rushed he, for all
to recall in hall new-hewed
from green hills' fair meagre heights,
won by raw fight's spear-borne feud.

Future kings' war sings ere sound
could fade, bound by war's cadence,
their gratitude exuding
awe-raising hue in years hence.

The Thorns on Life's Stem

Whence come the thorns on life's stem?
most of them, from holding back.
Fear to step forth to the fray
forfeits day to fortune's lack.

Opportunities abound
around the spring of one's years.
Hence peace accrues most for souls
who've reached for goals, shunned their fears.

No Rest for the Wicked

All mankind does fraily mends
askew ends, wild since childbirth.
Therefore, one strikes ore who asks
that our tasks teach us true worth.

Helpless Self-Disgust [*(c)*]

A tree's bark towers above
the tally of my allies.
Lack, on top when I looked up,
men deem a supreme surprise.

I thought I'd brought no debris
with me of youth's rage, ageless
pawn that I am, pushed onward
past roads long pain stirred, ease-less.

Fit I'm not (if it mean tall),
not quite wall-like, a wee lout
full-grown—unmown—now a man
whose upward span has pride's pout.

Ode to Alexandria

Alexandria, what tomes'
intense groans you evoke
from man's memory, proud nest
of the best the ancients spoke.

Tomes that covered science, gods,
how fate plods: what you preserved
was a past's glory that now
into sand's brow has since swerved,

lost to all time. Had you stood,
Serapeum, would our schools
not still be teaching the scrolls
whose rolls lined your walls? Mind drools!

Your days have sorely dimmed: sight
sees no more light from your isle
Pharos with fire's beam and ring
announcing *land near* with style.

There stood the Ptolemies' gem:
pliant stem of writings' bloom
swaying with the winds of thought
uplift wrought to rend man's gloom.

Interesting Times [*(c)*]

Troll-like crowd they near, louder
their laughter than ire, ill fit
to sway one's ear, entice ease,
or appease pain, aye, as it
swells close so lies can lace us
like porous shoes in oozing
mud whose false support's sudden
give makes sullen the living.

Nervous, the svelte seek shelter,
run helter-skelter, money
dwindling, ginned by trolls' swindling,
where we're mere kindling—eerie!
Be our windbreak, bard: *bar well*
this hell-disease blown breezeward.
Lash with awe; fell; unsheathe fire;
dry their mire with your mere word!

Cywydd Deuair Hirion

This is the one measure Gaels and Britons had in common, although each tradition embellishes it in a distinct way. I misunderstood it when I first tried it; by the time I did grasp it properly, I found myself primarily using the Irish version, *Deibhidhe*.

Merlin's Creed [*(c)*]

There are times, though rare, to muse
beyond what's fond (heart's refuse)
or weighed task (ere debts accuse)
or a wish (with *its* issues)

and chase (per pace apropos)
the unicorn: then echo
its call; stand tall; *sate* doubt; lowe[*]
as delight, then, adds tallow.

---

[*] a Scots expression (intransitive verb) meaning to 'flame, blaze, glow, light'

Warm Date [*(c)*]

A night's chill air notes each lure
that might give yen its tenure.
Need's demand aids a demure
frost to melt by imposture.

Man's Scrape [*~(c)*]

How shall I dub these troubles
(bemoaned) whose bright ebb man dulls,
this scrape we're in the Spinner
(Fate) must nudge, that feet may stir?

Lest complacent cue impede
going where truth has tarried,
follow every spark in full
and you'll find the plan ample.

The Condemned [*(c)*]

a noose dawns
        insidious
and kindly fuck
        this ruckus
to smithereens
        it smothers
my sail of fire's
        silver firs

which aspire to love's virus
still though will
        sought a lithe us
to tempt attempt more tortured
intentions
        (goal not assured)

Cyhydedd Fer

This measure is much like English tetrameter and so perhaps of a secondary interest; yet I seem to have produced quite a few examples, of varying quality.

The Big Sleep

"To sleep: perchance to dream," he said,
for life is waking, death the bed.
Perception's fog makes a mere dream
of life, hides the immortal gleam
we seem to sense we once all were
and sense we'll be again. The blur
at least allows adjustment's touch,
learn we little or learn we much.
The dream of death will 'rub it in',
make painful impress on our sin.
Life's where improvement must take place,
not death. In life we can *embrace*
its lessons, hoping our last thought
may lead the next life to what's sought.

To Cease Ill

Incessant Cecil B. DeMille
can't be good for you. The anvil
of time awaits the hammer's will
of when one's reduced to landfill
recurring-sound-wise, each oil spill
a sorish thumb. Can the anthill,
once constant verse fills the playbill,
use up all known consonance till
nothing's left for the whippoorwill?
Should one repeat? My codicil
says should that be so, I would chill
and try to make my output nil.

Turquoise by Day

Turquoise by day, lapis by night—
the former with its blobs of white,
the latter with its points of light—
this flattened orb's a stalagmite
in the dark cave of space, a blight
on the stark calm of the void's plight
in having only us to right
the wrongs of nature. Crisp insight
is needed. But instead, man's might
only undermines the upright,
turns truth's diamond into graphite—
like a pre-Moses Canaanite—
making day a feeble nightlight,
mankind in part a parasite.

We are the baby of the sky,
no more: stillborn, our throats are dry
from questioning exactly why
we must eat the *crust* of the pie
and leave the rest to vultures. Eye
of newt and toe of frog we'll try—

anything, lest our alibi
be compromised. Our efforts buy

no copper setting for the sun,
no silver setting for the one
whose star-points wink (where once was none,
if science be believed). They've won!
those spirits of ennui, who's fun
is tripping up thought's little run
of finding things to overcome
that won't be missed, such as reason.

Government [*(c)*]

In several nice average
neural sequences' mass passage
of whims to laws anew, sewage
has been building. Hose bone, bold edge:
the world of haste awaits wastage—
should we cry? Now hush, lad: carnage.

Bardic Secrets Revealed [*(c)*]

A bard's stand *divides* the landscape,
whose pairs assure his power's shape.
For straight back from eyes' horizon
points within, the tree of reason.
So concern shifts, seeks *inner*-shore
dominion. Air, pinion rapport
'twixt fate's tricks and thought's elixir,
so we clash not. Sky will usher
loot to nub if one draw substance
from fixed vision's grist, insistence.

The Male Tarantella

We drive the length that seeing goes
To spy the strength of being's throes
Under the microscope of shame,
Which thunder might yet hope to tame
Beyond the confines of today
And fondly con of love its say.

For there's no putting things aright
While cares' fond looking clings to night.
They lean on paws of loss unfair
Whom neon draws across the air.

You cry to drown marred sense of doom
While I impound barbed fences' loom
So we might weave our own display
And re-achieve the blown-away.

The upshot is this guilty plea:
The quiz whose cup is spilt is me!
Having lost the chance for freedom,
Lathered, tossed, I dance to *be* dumb.

The Poet Declares

most of today's poems consist
of platitudes—that I resist
(I'd rather be a satirist)
for I want sound to pierce the mist
that's around us like a blunt fist
otherwise one's just a rapist
of one's own time, own dime—desist!

when I'm gone I want to be missed
after all whom has the Muse kissed

Byr
a
Thoddaid

A quatrain utilizing the *gair cyrch* in one of its couplets.

Freestanding Byr a Thoddaid [*(c)*]

Assail tidy solitude—in lush warmth
now shall mirth be valued,
or hot as bed (how tea is brewed)
once night's chill turf has been curfewed.

Blessing's Might [*(c)*]

Take to wing, blessing: be all sound
a while, to be one whole tie bound
for better, free but around, calming stress,
claiming stray thoughts' playground.

Appeal to Self [*(c)*]

O reason, please arise now: piles
of tasks contrive to seek scant aisles.
Show moderation: *aim* then run—hell-bent.
Who'll bite? Foresight, for one.

The Cramped Present [*(c)*]

As Plato says, the present—most fleeting—
must float away, potent
yet dark (like space), one's fate latent
within its womb (the eye night sent).

Only what lasts glows, frozen—crystallized—
across it all, pollen
grown to flower: a grant fallen
at our feet and scooped up (eaten).

Spell for the New Paradigm (A Satire) [*(c)*]

The outer world, that rarely deigns
to note my lot or my quatrains,
stumbles, lost; nay ambles lanes—avenues—
that will bruise the tall brains.

And so this charm: crouch; look harmless;
ply your 'coy fool' ploy, nor confess
full value; urge feel of largesse—act lean.
Be seen a wreck, feckless.

Then shall blessings (thy shoal, o bliss)
from heaven course (firm heave, no kiss).
It's sky bears fruit, not trees' backs: axis *up*,
my cup awaits—make piss!

Clogyrnach

This measure has a kind of haunting quality that keeps calling me back to it.

Myrddin's Song Sung Before Gwenddoleu

In cross-hallowed halls, the south sits
dissembling, twisting things through lips'
wrinkled care, their cause
needled by new laws
whose curt claws
crack long whips.

By Lugh, light of the gods, do we
beyond the Wall, still fierce, still free,
oppose chains and choose
crisp battle's bare bruise,
lest one lose
wisdom's key.

In Praise of Rhydderch Hael of Strathclyde [*(c)*]

Sane is courage that sows increase:
a tough stride's pace to face tow'rds peace
forsaking fierce kin,
letting daylight in
so that sin seethe to cease.

Feed the Lark

How can the cream get to the top
of such vast mass of tomes, the slop
spilled from the lost mind
of those left behind:
can you find me a mop?

Surely destiny's hand will guide
my search so that the gems can't hide
from my grasping hand,
that my eye might land
somewhere grand thoughts reside.

Lead, cherished Muse, through forests stark
and gloomy to what rends the dark
haze hiding genius
from the omnibus
grasped and thus *feed* the lark.

Near Srebrenica

Orange the sun's departing show,
colorless the ridge's shadow,
for this valley's night
will have no more light
than the bright
searchlight's glow.

A depression, outlined with earth,
gapes from its having given birth
to that which explains
this region's dark stains
and its pains
of great dearth.

A vague scent pervades the still calm,
opposite of a healing balm,
unsavory stench
telling tales that wrench
hearts to clench
soothing psalm.

Something stirs out beyond the beams
with gentle yelping that redeems
the chill that descends
where a north wind wends
from the ends
of man's dreams.

A captain of artillery
asks of his guide if it might be
what has just been found
here beneath the ground
that such sound
seeks to see.

Scavengers? No: they belong here.
Their masters . . . there! A creeping tear
cuts short the reply.
Earth heaves a soft sigh
knowing why
dogs stay near.

Dark Music [*(c)*]

Let wind sigh its lament gently,
rude loss treasured, lest a rosy
sight dazzle study's
mood: brew mind a breeze
clouds' cold ease
fails to flee.

I've felt the calm of flute with key
unknown, a rambling worm ably
mending aim my doubt
can't shun, ache outshout,
borne about
sun's grim sea.

Ere sorrow age will I resurge;
heart yawns to swallow hurt eye's urge
to recall a track
followed (a fine lack):
a tense tack
dons wind's dirge.

Cywydd Llosgyrnog

Another stanza form that uses what the Irish call *aicill* rhyme.

Means Are Part of Ends

Decry atrocity forthwith,
at the base of the monolith,
    before the myth's clay is set
corrupting and encrypting ends,
forcing futures to make amends:
    life but lends what we beget.

Bran's and Krishna's Flute

Maker of calls I cannot make,
my lips being too glib to take
      the proper shape when they blow,
how plaintively your cries caress
the ear and calm a heart's distress:
      what blessing's boon you bestow!

Smoother of nerves in peace and strife,
big brother to the tinkly fife,
      you uplift life by your flight!
With throbbing pulse or pure clear tone
you laugh, you cry, you trill, you moan
      with lonely and fragile might.

Wind in the reeds, or bird in trees,
your music makes a gentle breeze:
      you please us with sifted air.
Speak to the ages, fair-voiced thing:
say to them, by the song you sing,
      "Soul take wing and shun despair!"

Tender Might [*(c)*]

Eye follows show, fall is unsure.
Need air seem lithe under some lure
      Love's enduring levees draw?
Caressing truth, care sang it right.
Soon came wan limbs sunk in moonlight,
      Tender might to dare my awe.

Fiddler's Hymn

Ah ta hear the drone o' the pipes
in the ring of the G from swipes
      of me bow, that likes to draw
the music of a warlike heart
from peaceful strains of ancient art
      in the part it plays for awe.

It awes me when I think the tones
that make the melody and drones
      are loans from a far-off time.
The music's feelings bridge the span
of ages since these notes began
      much better than pantomime.

Visions of heather, river, wood
that flourished where both bad and good
      ancestors stood I can see.
Air rings of graces of gaunt days
and pathos spawned by evil's ways
      in the lays they sing to me.

O magic thing of wood and gut
and horsehair through which the sounds strut
      in a glut of bloodly thrill,
serenely ears become engrossed
ta hear past ages' conjured ghost,
      an' I toast they ever will.

From the Fallen

I did not see the end of day:
some shrapnel took my soul away,
      out of man's fray to hell's fold.
Yet *knowing*, I'd have not hung back
nor bequeathed others, in my lack,
      death's honest tack to behold.

Better one be remembered well
and told of fondly in song's spell
        than dwell in dark vales of shame.
My effort was by duty drawn
and spent itself—love's willing pawn—
        for honor beyond mere name.

Celebrate not *my* driven choice,
to which these lines give fervent voice:
        rejoice for what souls my death
has kept preserved through battle's grind
who freedom's triumph hope to find,
        bought by mind and blood and breath.

Rhupunt

This is I think the oldest surviving strict measure, used in some of the oldest poetry that has survived. Rhyming a syllable not the last syllable of a word attracted me at first, but in the surviving verse I have read (not that I understand the early Welsh it is written in) the rhyme every four syllables was strictly end-word, last-syllable. Sensibilities being what they are though, it can sound a bit like children's verse.

Myrddin's Prayer [*(e)*]

Gifted god Luck,
shine on this muck
    men make of earth.
Your children flail
before a gale
    of gall, not worth.

Most who are left
are too bereft
    to lift woe's girth.
Help them to keep
their courage deep
    who mock in mirth.

Myrddin's First Winter in the Caledonian Wood [*(e)*]

Breeze turns to blight.
No ease at night.
Snow past knees' height—
    am I to freeze?
These don't seem fair:
swift flees the hare,
ice tombs seize hair,
    and bare the trees.

Old ways still sing
since bold hearts bring
swords' fire, molding
    torc's ring of gold.
Hold close the heat
whose fold is fleet
and warms cold feet
    where feats are told.

How These Times Look to a Man of the Old Way

Husbandry wanes; hollowness reigns;
    earth's blood congeals.
Let us not judge these times by sludge
    that was once fields.

The nymph-like stir to play *satyr*
    and spoil the spell.
Chiefs subsidize fatherless cries,
    manhood's death knell.

Paired providers, not nurturers:
    childhood has changed.
Replace firm trees with wild theories?
    Man is deranged!

When Times Are Tense [*(e)*]

Offer incense
to innocence
when times grow tense
     and treacherous.
All we abhor
unmasks us more,
cutting a core
     cantankerous.
Souls that succumb
and are nudged numb
appear fearsome—
     so pray for us!

Hardened

     rock
be like it
calm intrinsic
stiff upper lip
ice tough
     pre-lawn

     stone
an image
     not cartilage
reliant ledge
     or mean too long

     rock
intrinsic
     calm
me like it
scythe-proof
stiff lip
ice tough
     lovesong

Video Killed the Radio Star [*(e)*]

Insipid air
is everywhere,
insistent stare
  of the mundane.
It's trampled down
the dapper clown
of chance renown
  that was man's brain.
To modernize
the ill-earned prize
for silly eyes
  would seem a waste.
Incessant tries
at compromise
make butterflies
  by glass encased.
The forms remain
and forge a strain
of farmers' wain
  to be ignored.
It plods along
through odds' old throng
is what is wrong
  with that accord.
Today's ill song
by pill or bong
  is forced to thrive.
What of what's left
of lilt or heft
  can we revive!
I'll entertain
the winter train
  of my *own* fall
and catch no laughs
from hatched giraffes
  in my lone hall.

Measures Allowed the Chief Bard

The *Cyhydedd Hir* I start with was my first try at a traditional Celtic form: I added extra internal rhyme—I was not yet aware of the *cynghanedd* required of medieval court bards but sensed it should be ornamented. I soon learned *Cyhydedd Hir* and *Toddaid* were mainly used as variation in the *Cyhydedd Naw Ban* used by the chief bard. Many of the following use strict *cynghanedd*; a few utilize a more primitive pattern improvised by ear, as indicated below (and above) by [*(e)*] next to the title.

Straight Steps [*(e)*]
[*Cyhydedd Hir*]

Straight steps the cold bard from his hidden, hard
life in this bold shard of what once blazed.

Old recalled greatness these times miss much less
once mankind's late mess makes us amazed.

Still, with this deep call heard, though in dim fall,
words want to leap tall in flame unfazed.

Sift out the coarse drum's thrum—makes my ears numb!
Bran, let my horse come forth, songs be raised!

Autumn Facelift
[*'informal' Toddaid*]

The air of summer's vain with mere sorrows
whose blossoms appear gay, a poor gift
for one who wallows in life's rough hollows:
embrace what follows in fall's facelift.

Gwawdodyn of Self-Instruction [*(c)*]
[*an early effort, hence rather stiff and awkward*]

Rearrange sting's error, now unjust,
and fie, you'll see truth nod off; else trust
ill is deserved and lies' odes reave dust, dread
fled from point's edge, filed (firm pates adjust).

Set to, man: last time anyone looked,
if lot had boon, ire felt he'd been rooked!
Be counted among the booked, deeming *stain*
the *main* story hitched (though minced, re-hooked).

If you need a seer, find sorrow:
cause (sly fist, all ache) is self (stay low).
Rearrange sting's awry arrow: adjust
ingestion of tar for tomorrow.

Step Up, Poet [*~(c)*]

Cauldron-born of Ceridwen, carpenter
of song, stir now, voicing starry yen
to see sun's portal of hope open:
free feats' Luck today from fate's locked den.

Prayer to the Sun [*(c)*]

Sun, temper your rays for eyes gazing
at light's source, to allow it to sing
in their heart. Know the raw hurting—fire's stab—
besets anew us lab beasts' sole wing,
sight's sting. 'Twould be less curse than blessing
if 'twere capped, or *right* mapped your tempting.
We beseech you, teach in touching—to do
how Luna does when you lie dozing.

Once Bards Stood Second Only to Chiefs [*(c)*]
[*Cyhydedd Naw Ban*]

Sing tearful and long, with voice stronger
than wind, o bards, though day, now bearer
of noise, may hear you not, its poison
a silence in man's soul we summon
to fill your absence. Wit, flare beside
tongue's unbent powers, lent where praise lied
only till felled by satire's seldom
harmless breeze. You stilled seas! so told some
who lived then. Since do men cease demand
for words' full force: fair, our days fell fanned
into confusion's nest, hopes vested
in what great minds' calm heat once meted
unbecoming when foreseen bringing
comfort unearned. Ache! my fine, rotting
times: your wild, unschooled aim needs taming!

Ogam Consaine Speaks [*(c)*]
[*repeated consonants in calendar order (not sure what it means)*]

Able new fuss, billow no facile
heed to conquer how duty can quill.
Aim, gang (it's round). My gong *eats* sterile.

Can't Keep a Good Man Down [*(c)*]

What's fixated on heights, if cast down
may turn ruin's aim to rain renown.

Verse for the Screen 1: Cathen Tutors the Young Twins [*(c)*]
[*Scene: Druid Cathen lectures young Myrddin and his twin sister Gwyneth.*]

A druid's duty bids aid to boil
up from cup's core—poof!—or make peace coil
around one's staff. Raw need gnaws, so toil
hard: *tend* to this herd. Tied to the soil,
our aims sow uplift, prevent arms' spoil.
A locked fate one alone cannot foil:
you must tame the glib worm of turmoil.

Verse for the Screen 2: Lailoken Confronts Mungo & Entourage [*(c)*]

MUNGO:
Lowly I accuse wild Lailoken,
whose sail's tack shows his soul is taken.

LAILOKEN:
I bow not to threats, nor bait a thrust.
I seek knowledge still, scan all, adjust.
I bend, let cause mend ill-take as must.
I now find I'm my people's mind-trust.
I sue not for your god's stiff regard:
I wreathe a right gods are there to guard!
and I ken a haven men have marred.
Judge not, lest ye be judged for trudging
stooge-like, into a bard's ill-liking!

Myrddin's Mad Ravings upon Fleeing Arfderydd [*(c)*]

Lead us a path, wolf: I'll dance up it
with no complaint, though a camp well lit
stand in our way—where my great merit
(light within) might appear mere spirit
of brooding fear. We've borne a din fit
to addle a saint! Nigh done, we'll sit
for years and grab rest till it's habit.
But we must quash ebb. Eat mice! to quit
would aid nine enemies and admit
defeat. If you could nab a rabbit,
'twould feed us both, lest tide find ice bit
by hunger's fangs. Come, tree-bare summit:
I would brood up where dawn bared a pit
round me. Let world be light riled by wit.
Mood, writhe: taint made an unworthy tit
to suckle from with stance in transit.

Myrddin's Soliloquy [*(c)*]

Great chieftain, new-fallen, now few lines
that don your honor brave the confines
of song's cast, out there past the wry pines
whose tops mock my stock of mystic ire.
Long days filled with lays that fooled the lyre
of hope, lest need mope, lost, I admire.
A robed honor, pure, ebbed on your pyre!

Winds assist brazen lords of Christian
hosts field their ghosts, who failed the region.
Where gods bled, alack, head, look who won!
Who were then deemed high now writhe undone.
North's woods abhor their grisly portion.

Shattered mind, you once dined on sod deemed
hollowed ground. Now, your hall has bough-beamed
roof, floors rock-pinned, its wide walls wind-seamed.

Dear sister's wed to one who's meddling
in pasts' demise! a post so damning
because an accurs'd beacon (who's a king).
Mild-mannered man, his region spanning
strong-peopled hills, he'll leave deceiving
clues yet send many swords a-rending.

O Gwenddolau, your tall form falling
on battle's field, your men unyielding—
proud were we then, unpeered, unwrithing.

Myrddin Cringes from King Brother-in-Law [*(c)*]

Wreathe-Rick's about ere the irks abound.
Must hide for a spell from that hellhound.
Tears are afoot. A treasure I found
he'll sack! my filberts! (Be the background,
Mere-Then, safe from the hunt.) More than sound,
being seen in range is the danger.
Their arrows rip! (though rare is error
attendant on me, the far seer).
To hide! (Down, test.) At heed! (Do not stir.)
Surely I'd do well to find shelter.
If I hide, the hunt will range wider
and let me live. (Needle time, lover,
world a haystack without a tracker.)
Tomorrow may dawn (or I'm a goner).
I'll keep hope for now. Look up, hopper:
hop away, hare! for you're the bearer
of old lore in a world grown colder.

Myrddin Wyllt to His Estranged Wife

thinking of you I don't think
    much of you
my each avenue
    must bridge that brink
my own drive has spun
    this thread you kink

thinking of you I don't think much
    of *you*
I view
    our mating as youth's failed clutch
no
what I think of
    is your soft touch
life's hard in here
    with the beasts and such

Myrddin Compares Sunlight and Rain to Nothing at All [*(c)*]

Myrddin's the blight of his own nightmare,
piglet. Life's rigged! It reneged! Too rare
to verify aught over a fit,
but to have sun's rays beat heavy, sit
and writhe or else just endure the rain:
water cleanses peace; tear cools as pain
clears the field so we yield to a sign,
heaving sky's boon: having skin's benign!

The Poet's Art Has Waned [*(c)*]

Once we were schooled bards, so our psyches
obeyed raw power's bid: ear parries
poorly amid sun's peril mind sees
encroach foully on care each one flees.

Once words' force, marshaled, seared as if foe's
shield were lowered. Should our lyre now doze?
Do seers crawl? Day sours: key arrows
fall short of how far man sows sorrows.

The Spring Where Mere-Then Taught [*(e)*]

Is this Mere-Then's spring spouting wisdom,
moss'd wood of glens where the bard stood glum
when hard loss in war's toss left him numb?

Limbs' twist, in insistent witness, waives
words' speech long unheard in leeched enclaves
where Celts' gods, once knelt to, guard sod graves.

Spring, fluid mind: bring druid-mined truth
to earth's surface for worth's sake, that youth
might slake dearth of meat with thinking's tooth.

Song to Far-Off Times [*(c)*]

Folk of far-off times, mist which distance
innervates separates us who prance
each our distinct path. Charred sin tact put
in the running, fair though wrong, afoot
for all to see. True, free will eats us
by absence. Does force usurp surplus
in your day too? Of course; nor doubt it.
Did lack ride state back ere dust it bit?
Can Luck's flare repair it ere we pout,
knowing lobbying is all about?
Yes, in your world too, desire's truant
pyre, human, false, remains life's tyrant.

Memory's Firm Mire [*(c)*]

I will strive to harbor new lustrous
promptings, although a poor impetus
attend all but one not idle bit none
know save my own sun. The suave miss us
not, since we alone entice solace
from mem'ry's seat, whose firm mire gnaws us.

Forgive My Sarcasm [*(c)*]

What relevance: I hate to relive
verse whose pace is not quite abrasive.
I'll slow, I guess, let my aggressive
spirit, restored, separate restive
from high satire's good firm haste: rise! give
as good as got once girt, not furtive
sporadic sap—inflict speared ache's sieve!
(Bards are of late their breed's relative.)

Death of Archimedes [*(c)*]

Life lost as mind-tossed eyes aimed to stare
at an inscribed shape, to seek orbed share
of unfading truth's view, found to roar
where time's whisper mimes: hence paramour
of Light as ill Rome's night falls, now's alarms
ignored from choice that augured firm charms
at day's end, his greatness spared pending
he give his name, Rome's soldiers aiming
to take not kill, had fate been willing.

Tribal Invocation

In the icy predawn gathered they
there at the forest's core, their foray
bearing its whir of purpose towards day
as somber priests met the sun halfway.

Stillness is broken by intent. Words
mask meanings unfathomed by cowards.
The chief bard blesses the tribe's stewards,
those whose work brings an increase to herds.

Onset of light, onset of stirring
birds accompany the hymns they sing
to greet their great orb of gold bearing
life and light to the dark wood's hearing.

A tense sense of need fills this clearing.

War not of chiefs and oaths but of storm—
extermination—looms, legion-borne,
threatening end wherein none will mourn
except in chains, the world's fabric torn.

"God of groves, indifferent to man
save where unspoilt honor marks the span
of a whole heart, by your aid men *can*
become each like ten, each ten a clan.

"Weep not, god of strength: instead, bolster
these spurred spirits as we meet the cur
that nips at our tribe's heels. Death, deter
those chains that would enclose our power.

"We are freedom's voice in the forest
made of man, undeniably blessed
even if vanquished, since the gods' zest
flows in veins that flood to meet their test."

Grim history served to say the rest.

Under the Eaves

Life, why have you left me in this time
when English usage is in decline
(called archaic) and the paradigm
most on which our delving wits must dine
is dragged out from beneath pungent slime?

Dried out skies still starlit sparkle
      no more
      in mire
rooted and unmagical
which slime spawned as dreams delusional
in content and intent meant to lull
to sleep each grain of truth still supple.

Here beside the turning of these leaves,
why'm I left crouching under the eaves?

So Much for Moths [*(c)*]

seen descending from a sun dose nude
Icarus will join us
      lodge unwooed
amongst discards
      aiming sated
      skewed
as if a star
      it might be argued
a need
      eyed unenvied
      dawn unviewed

and the king's accountings continued

Own Your Karma

What's intended, sincerely thought—believed—
is heaved onto the karma pile, caught
in retribution's cyclic onslaught
that seeks to teach us but leaves untaught
those who think that fate's guards can be bought,
or by whom scapegoats are always sought
on whom to press blame for what fate brought:
this, man's greatest demon, brings to naught
all the pleasures for which he has fought.

Song to Myself

Who call it loss
      if a lone voice shakes
termite-etched pillars?
      Hark! it awakes,
this mire you stir
      with minor earthquakes—
and was Cassandra
      a jackanapes?

When Darkness Looms [*(c)*]

If counting sheep seeks sleep, success looms:
wool over eyes of lead in bedrooms.

The Head's Predicament [*(e)*]

Odd anyone could get heads to stick
on bodies such as these, where the trick
is to appease the trapeze fabric
to where it thinks you share its rubric
that it's all molecules time's mules kick,
not notions, and nothing is epic.

There is no greater pain-in-the-neck
than that round little ludicrous speck
making a body's life one spent wreck
by misdirecting it on some trek
after abstract facts it fain would check,
expecting flesh to just genuflect.

Said bloated head needs a neck that's stout
to hold it up as it bobs about,
boss to angels in its high hideout,
princely perch till earth's lurch asserts clout,
tells it how to hang and when to pout,
leading it by hand into its snout.

[*This was composed as satire directed against a poet who disliked me and was rude about it: he attended a poetry 'class' I was part of, and during the week following his hearing this satire he found himself compelled to move his domicile up the coast—good riddance! (Satire rocks!)*]

Rock! [*(c)*]

'Twixt toddler pebble and old boulder,
Rather than stare, herewith writhe astir!
Forth and back, songs' fiery thud obey!
Immobility's, alas, passé.

Sunlight on Water [*(e)*]

The sea angles down
        but edges up
into the air
        element it cut
off at the feet
        filling the great rut
the world is
        which is now a cup
        brimming
boar among beasts
        rooting out the muck

Insidious moisture infiltrates
atmosphere as it evaporates
disguises itself as air
        creates
weather everywhere
        and winters' aches
and it will until
        the world abates

Feel and Desire This! [*(c)*]

The mind is its own place, and in itself
Can make a Heav'n of Hell, a Hell of Heav'n.
    Milton (*Paradise Lost*, ll. 254-5)

In waves out of which the *now* spouted
(foul or pleasant) feel I ripples wed
to time's changing taunt, a maze each jest
of fate raises to taint the latest
dose of nature's dance. View chores anew.
Bid *one* desire *abide* dawn owes you,
to unify things. Wit, own faith in *wings*,
not in wanderings a toe would rue.

Cheap Seats Under Apple Boughs [*(e) & (c)*]
or I've Run Out of Give, Are You With Me?

Hind soon assays primed senses' pyramid
here amid alley cans and trances
indicative of, indigenous to
zoo-like circumflex circumstances
empiricism demands Kansas
take note of. Make a votive muck—of time,
of tomb, beaten vellum—but not of Luck:
that's where buck stops in this synopsis
for a tourist's view of the newness,
this 'give' our negative run got us.

Under the apple tree are we, arrows
rise but stick in the thicket thickly,
allowing us a breather to re-think
this thing, this stray stink sense, this shaky
perilous-feral-fuss-for-low-fee:
I've run out of give, are you with me?

[*the above composed the night my best friend died (unbeknownst to me), whose humor it reflects*]

The Alchemist's Prayer [*(c)*]

what self is
     is what flesh imprisons
as it seeks sleep's ease
     night asks lions
to punctuate pink
     chainy aeons
out of their centuries
     of reasons
and into shape
     andante aspens
or petite birch
     as if mere urchins

miffed
aether must sift
     thru misty suns

lead us not shocked
     into concoctions

Viking Thanatopsis [*(c)*]

Insufferable noose; fear; ebb; latched;
mortality a mere tail attached.
Foal, choice is the whole: chase as though hatched.
Fuss to suit, but be the fastest batched.

Shall time's impartial tombs map our isle?
whims' care mope? or stale wombs cramp our style?
Take to sea: a past spree posts *per rile*.
What's to come won't unnerve if servile.

Huge ache-toss looms? Then hijack its loaf!
'cquaint it with quantity: woo the oaf!
Tear-ified? detour, if a dead oath
split a hair to garb bare yet grab both.

Shun juxtaposition. Jokes tap ease.
Avoid the slop; avoid the poppies.
Think awe, energy: both can urge bees.
Fate's vice weaves the ice; waves, though, we seize.

Mortal Prospects

Death generates myriads of dreams
whose fixed face is not just what it seems.

The Mortal [*(c)*]

pompous
acephalous
      so a fail
it dies
ails otherwise
      lies there wail
note how *mean* my
      not-too-human male
the key
scrutiny
sick rut
      a nail
f'rev'ry shoe   love's
      fervor shall avail
not or send
the wind
      into your sail

rouse many (at best
      oarsmen) to bail
else expect rot   loss   aches
      pocked your tale!

Ditty

In any attempt to heal the wound
inflicted on the world by fecund
willfulness that has left it marooned
in caricatures of a harpooned
      whale
      who will
succeed must become attuned
to its prior state, that pristine-mooned
unsullied slate once it has been pruned
of wild growths by which it was entombed.

Bard as Throwback [*(e)*]

Bard as throwback punts his times
      into words
      not weird ahs
his stag of seven tines
still alive just grazing the confines
of his gaunt self
      whose inner outlines
are obsessed with the best paradigms

sealed inside a top half made of sky
something hungry stalks the how and why

but the paid experts claim otherwise
little do they know
      they have no eyes
but aim always outward
      pinned by size
seeing Luck as 'chance'
      not enterprise
redacted by half
      made of thin air
thirst distracted by the then and there

Words to the Not-So-Wise

I tell you, man,
      if you haven't learned
to laugh at yourself,
      then you're patterned
to live from rage to rage,
      taciturned
only by death,
      and poorly lanterned:
humor lets in light
      where pride gets burned.

How to See

I can see with the eyes of my mouth
       just so far
       like ravens looking south
till they dissolve
       and turn to spittle
in a bird's beak
       after the battle

I can see through the eye of my tongue
penetrating the cloud banks
       solemn
with self-importance
       yet never numb

or I can see you
       through this eyeball
that's left toothless
       in face of it all
see you as the window in my wall

N Trails

N trails
of human
       pathology
slime-ridden ruts
       in the sky's vast lee
tender an offer
       I must refuse
mind tries to rise above interviews
if when you are dancing
       the ants flatten
batten down hatches
       conceal your stance
ride the surface of the neutron star
through dream worlds of science's bazaar

Poet in Search of a Title (Croak) [~*(c)*]

Life's limbed fragile
      pinned to this frog pond,
reach curtailed,
      the raw itch care taloned
packed away.
Yet mind's need
      poked a wand
through the sky:
folded eye
      followed (dawned).

Feet plugged in thick mire,
      fight plagued new thought:
will the sink
now drink
      what wonder wrought?
A high tight noose seeks
      what toe once sought:
firm purchase
to yawn
      at mud's onslaught

Are You What You Are or What [*(c)*]
[phrase borrowed from Edie Bickell & New Bohemians]

      incomparable mouse
         a household
      unto himself
         not a home so old
      eyebrows grey as I browse
         gears' ebb rolled
      in neat package eyes
         on top cajoled
      with smiles to refresh
         wisdom's threshold

it's the house that's missing
      the singer
squeaks away
      sore that the great roarer
in the sky drowns him out
      the stouter
he is
that's showbiz
      thought's ash a burr
in the saddle
      of the battle-er

Co-Heed the Now-Bahn

I see myself
still try
      to impress
certain women I know
      go sleepless
at night that I might compose sweetness
for them to taste
with ear or face
      less
erstwhile urge
to burrow
      through a dress
than light that might be shed
      on the mess
my head is
because they are
      guileless
only to themselves:
      verse, make redress!

Over Many Lives [*(c)*]

bizarre and red ebb eyes rendered dull
by hints of forsaken principle
crowd pratfalls that would grow from woeful
to extinct while I blinked
      healable not
having got
      wisdom from a bottle

Poetry Is Composed by the Victors

The art and craft of poetry rests
on the art and craft of war.
      The pests
that threatened culture's nurturing nests
had to be vanquished first for fests
of the iambs and the anapests
to manifest our inner tempests.

Therefore should a poet praise
      warriors—
not the pompous, not falsifiers,
not the cruel,
      who relish terrors—
the strong! the upright!
      for this furthers
that stable stage where incanting stirs
subtle airs' sound-aquifers
      emerging
wealth which surging
      survival offers.

The View Ahead [*(c)*]

How I long to rise, a healing tree's
calm tower: view no calamities,
delve into work's broad live tracks—a breeze—
fly amongst tall trunks till a true ease
settle atop the forms life copies,
a new task up in want's canopies.

The Divil's Stopwatch [*(c)*]

Once our aim each hour meant so much more:
years' tinge maimed day's ruse to jam my door.

Griffon

I found myself being reached for! by claws
like lions' paws in size! and what's more,
a huge beak anticipating gore!
Its huge hindquarters were such as bore
resemblance to the king of beasts: lore
identifies just such motley store
of traits as *griffon*—dicey neighbor!
Not my notion of a fun rapport,
yet not a thing easy to ignore.

Her fur was tawny brownish gold ore
(her essence solar) as her claws tore
at mask's fabric as never before,
being a beast sprung from my own core—
embodiment of intense rancor.

You bet I quickly made for the door!

The Nine-Syllable Line [*(c)*]

The nine-syllable line slow-bellowed
by a bard in 'is hard nose-haired ode
must've been a boon back when winnowed
from its prose chaff to be the cathode
of thought's current's whir with brow furrowed.

Nine pulses pass whose stress their message
      carves
in curves as it swerves to ooze its wedge
through fear's hold on old ears: hailed a ledge,
this measure fed a poet's courage.

Just nine; but strict cynghanedd's dictates
upraised words from laggards: firm all gates!
lest song be lost
      slain by apostates
to sound faith in what grand sound mandates
in the new tall view it elevates.

The
Dark
Ages

The following are written in the style of the era of Aneirin (sixth century), based on the analysis of his poetry in *The Gododdin of Aneirin: Text and Context from Dark-Age North Britain*, edited by John T. Koch. The lines do not adhere to strict syllable counts; the only rule seemed to be avoidance of 13-syllable lines (whether from thinking the number unlucky or from knowledge its taboo status stems from holiness, I know not). The poems below are embellished much as the original lines of the *Gododdin* were: internally rhymed syllables with added consonance, a term often taken to mean consonant-agreement but technically meaning an *agreement in more than one sound* ('sounding together') that yet may fall short of rhyme. I love the greater freedom this style affords, as it allows the ear alone to determine things.

The Intermeshed Strands of Thought's Force

We are all sorcerers,
whose source of power stirs
    will's vapors from mere whims.
Our times have hid from thought
that which thinking wrought
    but we're caught in its limbs.

In the Style of Old Britain

Wood, be of oak,
oak of bright bolts:
bolts, bring your fire,
fire that makes royal,
royal need of bards
bards bend to hear,
here where want calls
calls peeped bird-like
like wisdom's bait
set to snare those whose glare truth would sate.

A Twist on Cyrch Gymeriad

coolness itself—
self's self-centered
interred-in-guilt
gilt mound of earth
worth naught mention—
shunned me still

till hummed this page
rage has as nave
engraved tranquil

quill we call work
as we 'work' others
(udders dripping
gripping kindness)
mind nests beside
your bedside skill

swill (in these airs
arrogance stirs)
stars' mute trickle

Miscreant Mimicry

[Inspired by Dylan Thomas's "Fern Hill"]

you can forgive the glintings of moved steel-like
passages in pieces pounded into blight
of the long haul boasted of beyond insight
or one or more of things lore means gathered tight
tied up in a ball as if they were alright
with their withering calm allayed sunwise by night

still flesh to mill about must leave its lean pallet
water sparkling savory in the spilled day yet—pleasant
miscreant mimicry seeking to become ably hep
to the short stick grabbed at quick by some Imhotep
hidden amongst grasses with the adders and wet
as will admit clods' softened heads as an asset

very astute winnings this as he sings to eat
and eats to sing heart taking wing for the wild feat
of flying solo through so low a life elite
but misestablished tablet from the high heap
after Babel and the dense yet winsome well of the fleet
and hip that hop on all threes not lame but deep

Finding Inspiration in Form and Sound

Are poets wise to scorn sound-craft's ear array?
What can prose chopped into lines topped
     by a title convey?
How much more attuned to art's foray
to seek to gird words' wee girth with dismay,
raise its worth above rays of the everyday,
of a simple sun, to a sound complex as star-play
     as it stirs cunningly
     and whirs with Faraday.

Internal Strife

Bright the sunlight flashes on rash steel
      to bid me beat down the unreal.
Bright the hordes of phantom lords that feel
      my strokes' shadows as blows to their keel.
Bright the roots of rage in me congeal.
Bright was life till loss made its appeal.
Dark now, my dragon prow divides waves.
Dark sea-troughs I plow, as pride craves
      vengeance on dreams desire deems want's slaves.
Dark the mood Satan's brood in me braves!
Dark, my eager anger ill-behaves.
Dark the straw-man stories label knaves
      whose swelled blood dries in craving's caves.

To "Somebody That I Used to Know" & "Boys of Summer"

      odd I can feel
      feelings from youth
      youthful and strong
      stronger far now
      now that the hunt
      hunts me no more
      haunted not by what the hunt is for

      for I *will* thus
      thus mind is clear
      clear to the edgy
      edge of the sound
      sounding my depths
      depths once dormant
      not dormant now
      now having passed
      past one whose range
      ranges to odd
      me I'm not your average sod

Bardic Lore and the Love Unlike Lust

Culled in the womb of days, it dawned undaunted.
Its long gestation hidden, it had adjusted.
Of a kind not common kindled it heart and head.
And feet followed where that love led.
Of brooding understanding was it bred.
It seems its wonder must sing to be fed.

Its work is art,
its art power:
power to sway
and assuage wrong
      with song and harping.
Its closing one in has freedom's ring.

Lugh's Face in the Far North?

Loki was cloaked and crafty: craft he had.
Odds and ends he got made the gods glad
till on balance his challenge made them mostly mad
over that folderol of Baldr's fall, so sad,
and thus rather dramatically he was branded bad.

Thomas à Becket

Man of the cloth—motley meek martyr indeed!
Martyr to the haughtiness of his false creed
that no priest might answer for a heinous deed
to the king's law, from moral sense atrophied
by the cheap partisan pull of petty greed
for power and protection unsullied
by reason's force, which faith's recourse dare not heed
and yet remain vital to human need:
I'll *buy* him the bucket in which to bleed!

Arfderydd (573)

Birds bear witness there were tense moments wrought.
At the dyke Dreon's band hounded those who floundered
      as they crossed and were caught,
those Christian lords with their mixed hordes, a hard onslaught.
Though weight won out, dearly was flood and near bank with blood bought.
Then Gwenddolau's host, with shields foremost,
      faced hours fraught with hazard
as wizard Myrddin spewed dark words spurred
      by what the foe sought,
those sons of Elifer sent to confer faith on those whom the gods taught!
With war's whine were lines joined and new meaning coined
      for the word *fought*.

Urien's peer,[*] chief champion of the old belief
      fell with a shout.
Under impetus of Cynfelin the Leprous
      and Dunawd the Stout
and Gwrgi and Peredur, sons of Elifer,
      did it come about,
all of whom horse Corvan bore to seek out
how Myrddin's war fog cast its bog of doubt
(to which horse was immune). Numbers soon
      claimed their clout.
Men of the old ways fell back, dazed
      yet 'twas no rout.

Behind thick walls their angry calls rang
      defiant and loud.
Never to yield that newly hallowed
      field they vowed.
Given the loss of a chief
      most retinues bowed.
These were uncontrite a month and fortnight
      till by death cowed.
They *were* their chief's famous chess set
      that played itself, still proud.

----

[*] Gwenddolau

The bard Myrddin, once so certain,
       was now by spell's failure awed.
Infinitely sad
driven half mad
       at his hair he clawed
wandering unblessed
through thick forest
       his lost lord to laud.
There I found him
of whom I am fond
       once climate had thawed.

His twin sister, wed to Strathclyde's lord—
their son lost as battle's cost
       her heart ignored,
that by sister's succor might mind be restored
and allow *Lailoken*—'twin brother'—to teach
       by his spring, from the mind-hoard
of the old way, from that whence
Bran's cauldron's contents
       were once poured.

The Afterground

The afterground of battle—whose baffled cries
from the near past form the far post of battered lies
spun around who won or what defeat's hope buys—
steams in mourning's sun, warming blood as it dries,
evaporating to chase the receding mist in eyes
left open frozen in their crisp demise.

How might heal the wounds zeal inflicts on enterprise
in echo to the false waltz of the unwise?
Flood said field, death's lake—our afterground, our wake—
       with new surmise, o gods,
though odds are you second this bizarre exercise
to further ends envisioned through a lens of flies.

Be the Bearer, Not the Load

Only in some salient and translucent moment may we enter
the sanctum deepest in us and test the pathway thither.
The wise may find that they don't mind the weightier
high-maintenance fronts this opens, and once the first shock is over
an ever growing gain in strength reveal and in others stir
that would have gone begging in the preceding lull of a winter
self-imposed to seal off the implausible, which seems now nearer.
Be not the bitter load but its bright bearer.

As I Walked Out in the Woods One Day

As I walked out in the woods one day, to escape
the foibles of the fur-challenged ape
and his concrete byways, my exposed nape
(it being a summer's day) found hairs agape
and stiff when the eyes it held up fell on a lake
with a lady's arm extending out of it like a stake,
offering an ancient and corroded sword for me to take
back with me where it would only create a stir and make
getting home without its being confiscated an innate
improbability. So I just stood there, wishing the State
and its restrictions didn't extend to this break
in the trees but stopped at the last house I'd passed late
that morning when headed out into the great
beyond. All this passed in a flash, then my plate
became even fuller, for the arm kept extending straight
towards where I stood, revealing first a face whose shape
drew me, then shoulders of a smoothness that might slake
one's thirst for pulchritude, then more! as the cake
appeared and I watched her pale breasts rake
the water as she stepped forth leaving her wake
behind her to step out onto the shore and shake
the moisture off her raven hair, whereupon Fate
intervened: she saw me, and ere she might sate
my curiosity (running high) she displayed the trait
of skittishness (having no doubt surmised I rate

nothing in her world or mine) and with an intake
of breath vanished utterly, causing me to quake
with amazement! She left but a single flake
cast off from the scales of her tails, and heartache
on my part for what might have been had I the bait
to catch such a prize on my line for love's sake.
Ah, well, that's the way life sometimes will drape
when tailored by Trickster, from whom there's no escape.

Spirit of the Era

You equate modern with advanced—as if all time
like concrete slime went only forward enhanced
each step by whatever way feet have danced
past sundry wars plagues catastrophes countenanced
by powers that be . . . in order to be entranced?
You carry on about a hum-drum sun long-lived
yet vacuous since it's appetite is contrived
to make it so . . . my, how thinking has writhed
in anguish over emptiness making it full
of itself and of uncertainties less ample.

Modernity's Mighty Fall

In the inclement slough of life's scaly waste
art arrays choice errors, as if chased
by youth's demon fist past oath's demands: fast-paced,
it's coldly slowed once the crux of a question's faced.
That's the kind of stir with which the ledger's laced.
Is lack *worth* its ode being lies, like earth debased?
The repute words' flagrant rapture, now fallen, graced
awaits us all, each goal a tall twitch of haste.
There energy's emptiness empties, unerased.
There the poet's chair is in its own glow encased.

The Advantage of Having Gone Through the Door

I am youth itself
      next to the young
who age in my presence
      I hold my tongue
untouched by time in silence
while wallowing in penitence
for I must stand for things that matter
that a glossy lens fails to register

Book of Acid (To a Prankster)

Seen in the far haze, as on faeries' looms,
an interlaced agreement's traced 'twixt lines and tunes
favored by bell-bottomed throngs
      like brides and grooms
that make a hieros gamos out of rock cartoons:
urban and antediluvian gather the fair fumes
as art's soft petals part
      and love's flower blooms.

Lead me by the hand, gentle command,
      past cold glooms
whose eyes the stance of a chimpanzee assumes.
Level me! Lift up all that sup
      on noons of days.
Spread out ways all at once ere head resumes
collecting seconds that lead to tombs
of times beyond some far-off kind of mushrooms.
The forest creatures have found the compressed
      essence that dooms
grey claims of everyday chains
      where night looms.

Yes, but Where Did I Leave My Mind?

It is only an inconsiderable mess
this tidbit of stress the world's been under
since its insidious loss of wonder
at the architectural marvel the stars were
once it was made out they as little matter
as individuals as do we since larger
fields are afoot of a meaning lesser
even than the mote on a throw of dice cups in amber
frozen long ago in the pose of a dancer
in this ballet of the melodramatic whir
that has danced quiet agonies to peals of thunder
since Adam was a schoolboy and earth much cooler
then than now and anyhow we didn't fool 'er
she sank into the gold where we couldn't tool 'er
and contemplated giving back the rib as a spoiler
what was it that was her name
night
or something similar

The Sea Wall

Image: one thin crust must stand against the moisture.
Built so long ago no song's sung of its tenure.
Lost the forgotten tunes, brittle and pure,
animating arms to wield weapons' cure.
"No savagery past this point," legions assure.
Which side of the barricade, brother, might be *your*
pumpkin patch where you hatch your lure, your plot?
Everyone's got at least one to manicure
or mask to smuggle past public censure.
Ours, as it turns out, is to endure.

Reluctant Optimist

Alas, let us join this drudgerous day
which no mere glittering night of lust's spent might might allay
the weight of (if man's crass fate has its way).
Yes, by making the best of things, man's behest
     has its say as well,
enough to tell air and the ground around us just what may.
For thoughts we bring near seep
     clear into the clay.

Envision Victory

Dwell on defeat and you will feel depleted,
and that will lead to being defeated.
Has not fate been clear? It is the spirited
who prevail over lethargy's dread.
Fortune's maid is to raw courage wed.

A Poet's Life

I always took it for granted I was the best poet in town
from the moment I was full grown and had it down
I'd have my mouthed words crown
     their own
sovereign throne
     resonating without renown
nor need of string, skin, flute, nor ring of notes found
fully formed in the fount of song counted on to frame the foreground.
A poet, he will look you in the eye, his eyes a pack of hounds,
and make you see what you entomb and treasure in your tall mounds.

Confession

I do not *write* poetry: I *compose* it.
It's just that while a poem is in transit
to others' mouths, one must apply one's wit
to arranging the words that flow forth so they fit
comfortably on a page, to become the bit
that reins in someone else's speech to benefit
from this talent I was born with in my kit—
which also includes that of fiddling twit
in a pinch, and of course thinker of merit
(unrecognized but real), my mind being well lit.

At least I don't have to worry that they'll audit
my finances anytime soon, since the chit
I earn from such talents (once treasured) does credit
to Diogenes by imitating his quaint habit
of unabashed homelessness, his sly gambit
to garner attention and show the deficit
he rated the world as. Indeed what I posit
as answers to problems the world's great flaws emit—
from which we may *not* run away like a rabbit
but rather must weather wherever we sit—
will surely earn me plaudit after plaudit . . .
> except I'm not
> anyone
> you can edit.

Poverty of Spirit Is Worse Than Poverty of Gold

> cash is king
> its kingdom want
> its girth a gaunt
> gauntlet of touch
> its touch a packed
> glove of contact
> tactile schemes
> half sense half dreams

their seams piercing
singing's calm
a bed of lies
lies ahead
if head aspires
with esprit gone

As Buddha or Iesus Might Admonish Us

Once the key that can crack wide
the gate that leads to less suffering
        surfaces
        interstices
between rocks' thorns become the thing
        that gives shelter
not the rocks themselves that can bring
ruin or block the view of what they're harboring.

Know you not what brand of candid
show-and-tell bestowed such squalid
handiwork on this hive of avid
busybody bees that your fierce fetid
inner wound has you as an invalid
among sentients? Nature's a scouring squid
whose tentacles are on man now
        for what he did.

He chose outer
over inner
and built nature
        a pyramid
at the bottom
of the aquarium that
        thought's
        thick
        ink
        hid.

Mixtures
of
Forms

Typically intended for the screen, the following each involve more than one form, often a mixture of Irish and Welsh, as in dialogue involving Irish and Welsh poets.

The Pyramid's Leaden Peak: A Chief-Satire [*(c)*]

Insistent airs sustain it
for mists so spare in merit
to thus meet at the summit.

Insistent whims sustain it: gone awry
on the fly, how they flit—
late, layabout—all a tall bit
of loony effort, vile, unfit.
Insistent ears sustain it. Gone awry—
gone bye-bye!—on the fly, now they flit—
alight about—in an elite bit
of aligned effeteness, a veiled fit
consistent aim can stain not
(truth's passport to wrath's pisspot).

Verse for the Screen 3: Blaise Instructs Merlin

[Scene: Merlin's teacher, BLAZE (called in romances 'Blaise'), teaches the child prodigy.]

BLAZE
This isle holds keys to mysteries that open eyes.

MERLIN
The tree-letters, and the numbers they symbolize . . .

BLAZE
some open, some in stealth—great wealth! Wisdom's prize
preserved since earth swerved and unnerved seas quashed man's cries.
        [sweeps horizon with hand]
Our great Cauldron has *two* rims: one, the far horizon—what the eyes find—
and what's straight back from that rim's track and points behind.

MERLIN *[after pause]*
Myself! Within! I knew! I win! You mean the mind.
        [tries to roll his eyes up and around to look 'within']

BLAZE
Without runs deep: it is oak's sweep; midsummer's heap; the hero's cairn.
        [tousles boy's hair]
Beneath that thatch, *within* must match its depth and hatch a serpent's bairn.
First the year's birth from whitened earth or winter's dearth, that cause for mirth we number *five*:
the midwife sits and counts digits while hand fidgets with new limits, being alive.
It is the birch—purity's perch—which in the lurch we must besmirch just to survive.
Prophecy's seen the future lean on *five* to clean: that which whitens.[*]
It would appear what we hold dear comes from the clear thoughts of titans.

[Scene shifts: 7-year-old Merlin, who appears ten, being led towards the overlord Vortigern]

MERLIN *[voiceover]*
Were they taller than us, master?

BLAZE *[voiceover]*
Taller within, perhaps; wits faster.
But their grand age met with disaster.

---

[*] (boron, atomic number *five*, whose ore is borax)

MERLIN [*voiceover*]
Perhaps they fled 'within', then used plaster
to seal it closed, like a spell-caster!

BLAZE [*voiceover*]
What they did, my avid Mer*l*inus,
was hide keys in trees: we make a fuss
over sounds; but this ground's perilous,
since few grasp how truth's clasp can save us.

MERLIN [*voiceover*]
I know my task in life: I ask your wise guidance.
Stay by my side: I've a wild ride to prominence.
Instruct me well, for I'ill compel wide allegiance.

BLAZE [*voiceover*]
Oh yes, I sense this in you, hence: count me servant.
(May your widened mind once ripened be as fervent.)

[*Merlin and his captors finally reach Vortigern, at the site of his would-be stronghold.*]

Verse for the Screen 4: Merlin Meets an Irish Warrior-Poet

[*Scene immediately following Merlin Ambrosius's confrontation with Vortigern and his druids.*]

IRISH BARD:
Wit 'twere bard yuh'd be, young lad,
had I a hand's width in it.
You've poise to face readied wrath,
path steadied by wide-eyed wit.

MERLIN:
For me they recruit austere tutors:
I attest bards make the best teachers.
        [*smiles*]
I sing englynion on osiers praising
the amazing din that leads inwards.

IRISH BARD:
Youth's no safe shield with oath's robe in tatters.
What matters is that a mind can probe
and get a solid grip on the globe—
grab its dragon by the odd earlobe.
Deep-welled aims kept within home's hedge-guards
saved us Gaels from Rome's scheduled schoolyards.

MERLIN [*to the distance*]:
Though girt gloom the great goal mar, come what will,
there leads Britain still, the world's bright star.
Great Annwfn's joy grew tin in 'is jar—loan
grown to help men stand on their sandbar.
I'm a Roman . . . *and* a Briton,
born to frighten girls from afar. [*smiles*]

IRISH BARD [*grasps his right arm*]:
Ever your fierce follower;
your call be my time's tether.
Fly, fellow well-wallower:
I will be honored ever.

Verse for the Screen 5: Arthur Seeks a Second Wife

[*Arthur, with Merlin Ambrosius, leads knights north towards Carlisle to wed Guinevere.*]

ARTHUR:
You know I fancy that lass.
And she seemed antsy for *my* ass!

MERLIN AMBROSIUS:
Leave lines to me: your tendency to revelry makes your speech crass.
What you call verse only gets worse: call for a hearse! go and say mass.
You must build strength throughout the length of your kingdom.
It's hardly news whom you must choose: win some, lose some.
   (*grins*)
Let's go beguile hearty Carlisle. Smile. Don't be glum.

Verse for the Screen 6: Arthur's Speech to His Knights

[*Scene: Artorius addresses his 'knights' (Sarmatio-British heavy horse) before the battle of the Caledonian Wood (late 450s), a speech composed for him by his mentor Merlin Ambrosius.*]

Freedom, for some, is fearsome . . . [*some laugh*]
an unkempt mind the symptom. [*more laugh*]
Having that inner kingdom—thought's domain—
to reign in, they turn dumb.
     [*some chuckle and comment*]
We're Britons! [*a cheer*] We're *born* at odds
with ire sent from other sods
where they adore strange war-gods—to enslave
the brave, here, by their rods.
     [*a few yell curses*]
They err! [*cheer*] We stir. [*cheer*] Advance and set right
this threat out of the north: be forthright!
     [*a roaring cheer as he leads them off*]

Verse for the Screen 7: Myrddin Asserts His Authority

COURT POET:
Look at what the cat dragged in!
Claims can tell us where and when.
Gentlemen, this man's mere then!

MYRDDIN:
Some as slaves fare. Seems an ass lives free!
Can you guess why nature's so messy?
Who is chief bard? one unschooled? hardly!
I, though mere apprentice, am clearly,
I fear, teacher here, to a chair high
and heaving born, kneading brain and I.
Takes pains, they'll know, to expose the lie.
Fools rarely speak safely, speck, so fly!

[COURT POET *visibly shrinks and slinks away*]

The Long View

[Narrator's summation at the end]

Over the long term, destiny
can reek of stark futility.
Arthur bled to keep Britons free
which later lured calamity
when trade brought plague from Rome's dark sea

a trade shunned by the savage Saxons,
hence future skies yielded English suns.
But look: inside the generations
are individuals, not minions.
Some learn, some burn, all preparations
for new lives to be lived, the stout rungs
on Light's ladder, roadway of truth's tongues.

No, the long term is not the long view.
For that, you need to look within you.

For Love
of the
Gaels

*English-Language Poet Utilizes
the Traditional Irish Measures*

Tarry
[Rannaigheacht Bheag]

Tarry long, maid of mindful
song, and ferry heart's handle
across chasms egged idle
by prideful thought's ebbed angle.

Graze, eyes once held now hidden,
jelled glib in ways of women.
Cradle softly spun silken
tongue: lilt in lofty linen.

Faith, test life's likely limits:
crave zest, like feisty ferrets.
Buttress weal with spruced spirits' boost
       near its means' merits.

Prime the scene for charm's cheeky
ways—arms that preen don't parry.
Clasp a tone bold and breezy
grown easy, tasked to tarry.

Rannaigheacht Bheag

When first exploring *Rannaigheacht Bheag* I worked from modern specifications that did not require rhyme (even *Irish*), only consonance. My main interest leans towards older specs (modern usually means *easier*). "Tarry", above, is old school, as are the last one or two below. The rest are óglachas and I am sure fall short of Dán Díreach. "Money" utilizes alternating 8- and 6-syllable lines (modern specs).

Faraway Voice

Softness of mouth and manner
housed in her breathless banter
makes my lonely pulse patter
with ache its only answer.

Another's warm hearth harbors
her loved form—art *my* ardor,
rift-born thoughts my angst's arbor:
trees' star-wrought gift I garner.

Empty air's roar is raucous;
wind pairs her with poor plaudits.
Storm's choice uplifts what's lauded,
warmth's voice that sifts through softness.

Power's Poles

White bishop and black bishop:
light and lack divide vision.
Pure light, pure dark, sounds simple:
allure's bounds wall-in wisdom.

To wield only one? Witless!
Half the field shunned—how shiftless!
Give back my might this minute,
white bishop *and* black bishop!

Ramparts of Montségur

Time's broad haze beholds ramparts
manned bravely—the bold Cathars,
their cleansed souls a voiced vanguard,
their tense choice, to stand stalwart.

Stirred to protect bashed borders,
God's elect just weren't warriors.
Yet they inspired spent forces
sent to guard freedom's fortress.

Fly, faith: resist where driven,
in mists' uplands, high, hidden.
Tow'rds this strong base were bidden
a chased throng, shrunken, shriveled.

Time recounts what lurked below
climbed and curbed that mount remote.
Hate's blaze, loud and vile, revoked
lives that time's broad haze beholds.

Money

Money, molten blood of culture's
    flood of fun and ulcers
needed for repair of punctures,
    there to seed our suppers.

All-pervading fuel of fortune's
    call, or tool of tortures:
with it, older guys buy gorgeous
    wives both cold and cordial.

Who is born in business clumsy
    must rue the norm numbly—
such as I, whose gift is grumbling,
    miffed, mumbling of money.

Valentine's Day

Eyes glowing and lark lurking,
rowing prize faith forth flirting
with disaster, n'yet yearning—
stiff afterwards, head hurting.

Prime passed sees a nerd ponder
still, quite the unsure shopper.
Tart youth was a force fonder
of coarse spoof, inhaled hotter.

Day, let loose harmed hearts' havoc:
use enchantment's charmed attic.
Head aglow and face frantic,
egg-on grace to stow static.

Man is made to choose, homing
on two main modes of 'knowing':
wise above, but groin groaning—
dove's dawn, with glazed eyes glowing.

Wring Out the Old

Wring out the old sun's cycle.
Cold numbs its spring of spittle.
Past's fool evades what's vital:
school fades like a raft's ripple.

Restive hopes stalk the stolid.
Festive talk totes the tepid.
Ring out the square and squalid.
Sting, tall id: flout the fetid.

Seems best one live a little,
sift dreams, contest their title.
Our once bold fling is fickle:
wring out the old sun's cycle.

Rannaigheacht Ghairid

An early love of mine, this form still draws my interest, for the way it commences.
I do not know if this measure is even included in Dán Díreach, but it has its appeal.

To Inhale

To inhale
means to palpably impale
mem'ry's face on that fragrant
scent fate's vagrant cuts curtail.

I bewail
her distance. The dire travail
her exhalations engraved
I, enslaved, ache to inhale.

Oak Gawain and the Holly Green Giant

Holly king,
your axe falls less threatening
than fear itself would have lain
on Gawain, had he fear's sting.

Brothers true
you remain, being the two
halves of the sun, the twin sons
of her who runs with the dew.

Lady moon
bore you both in winter gloom
at Yule: god and giant vie
to be high king of spring's tune.

Holly lost.
Thus must giant field the cost
to test his brother, the oak,
by blade's stroke, him born in frost.

Oak, steadfast
through cold winter's chill, must last
to reign over pollen's bloom,
then in summer's tomb be cast.

Who'd endure
knowing death is the last lure
without that test of tongue's blade
by brother laid, pointed, pure?

Hero, sing,
stout spirit unwavering
till spring's foredoomed end, which grants
summer's plants their holly king.

Got Too High

Dad makes wings,
gives me two of the damned things,
but then it gets out of hand:
when I land short, guess who sings!

Gods, who lurk,
put the fat lady to work,
her song bringing to an end
your old friend me, the real jerk.

By wing'd cape
two of us try to escape
from Crete: sun's heat unwaxed me,
and the sea was there to gape.

Cast no blame,
though, on dad: mine is the shame.
Must've gotten way too high
for men to fly—down I came!

Don't be sad:
you see, not even I'm mad
since I'm mourned by three nice girls
wearing only curls—plus dad.

Trilogy: Gaels at War

1. Come what may

Come what may
the horse I rode to this fray
that's carried herself an' me
nobly, her I'll ride away,

come what may.

2. Paean to a Fallen Youth

Gallant lad:
fervent as thunder, he had
ev'ry intention o' be'n'
seen ta servive battle's mad

rush. Claymore
whirlin' deftly, wounded sore,
he stopped fer no nap an' bent
all 'e wuz sent from God's door

on the spent
foe, near breakin', a well-meant
act even though we'd a won
had 'e not done—true gallant!

3. An Irish Adventurer Fights with the Swiss

We stood, pike
an' halberd formed in rows like
boar bristles. Soon Austrian
horse an' foot ran at our dyke

like the sea.
Steadfast muscle-thrust stood we
choppin' up their gizzards fair
that sought, ere the Swiss be free,

ta die, good
soldiers all—not made o' wood
but soon quite stiff nonetheless.
Ta give 'em rest, there we stood.

Pferyllt's Prayer

azure rain
clutters the sky's cloudless lane
sun's clarity tritely tinged
light's glow has impinged on pain

o black breeze
inkblot out all but the knees
one's brought to by regret's path
the wrath of past travesties

one's child-soul
seems ivory yet the toll
of old lives' woe weighs it down
as its thorn'd crown and its shoal

good red road
that leads beyond yearning's goad
point purpose to the hard test
where light's quest is truth's abode

silver wheel
projecting what was deemed real
that made the inner realm loom
adorn doom with your appeal

while soft gold
strewn on ground that's growing cold
puts poultice to poet's voice
rejoicing in visions bold

silv'ry grain
whose spark of light is my gain
sprout the rays that comprehend
and transcend this azure rain

Idols

Idols raised
in worship, in olden days,
though priests meant them as life's chains,
repaid man's pains in the praise

given sound
symbols often in them found
useful to the mob that strives
to live lives that are thus bound.

Truth's a sieve:
life's tidbits, all relative,
sorted by life's absolutes,
show the roots of what we live.

Idols served
other ends too, that deserved
less respect than that received
from the deceived and unnerved.

Some were fed
human blood by souls so bled
of gentleness as to think
gods that drink it worth the dread.

In that light
today's idols hide from sight
and don't directly gulp blood,
yet that flood is still our blight.

Truth is grazed
at times by religions' dazed
echo of Truth in what's taught,
but Truth's not in idols raised.

Morning Dew

Morning dew
dawns adorning thoughts of you
that night has left, leaving lots
of grieving spots bright in hue.

Drink up, air,
that which sun will shrink, not share,
one sparkling moment, no more,
show meant to adore and dare.

The sun yawns
over feelings flung on lawns
by light's storming of love's lair
there where the morning dew dawns.

L o n g . . .

in compost,
part of what I am is toast,
not much use in soil's rebirth
and not worth what it once grossed.

Lacking bread,
my voice gums bold words instead;
seeking purchase on the wind,
these rescind what storms have said.

Toothless song,
transmelodious and wrong
for some, still it preserves rich
ashes for which day's wastes long.

Lone I Thrive

Lone I thrive
and won't just take a swan dive
like a boat that needs a fleet,
social sheep hemmed by the hive.

Inner thrills
mean my thinner throng fulfills,
by meek design's deft desire:
my warm fire outshines their frills.

My thoughts probe
from undistracted brain lobe
deep mysteries that resist
minds still kissed by taming's toad.

None will groan
when I pay back this starred stone,
yet I'll have gained more than they
in the way that we're *all* 'lone'.

Rannaigheacht Mhor

I wrote quite a few in this form: since it is named the 'Great Versification', I took it very seriously, early efforts based on modern specs requiring only 'consonance' (in the scheme a-b-a-b), later drifting towards rhyme. Irish rhyme of course allows substitution of like-sounding consonants (*p-t-k, f-th, m-n-ng,* etc.).

Young Ballerina In the Wings

In the wings, waiting to fly
yet shaking, she lightly leans.
Her shoulder stills her, till stride
takes her, bolder, where pride preens.

Tense her thoughts, for thrill's great weight:
soon to fulfill, first it vents.
Then, with poise pulled forth, not faked,
noise and ache won't upset sense.

Seconds pass, then comes the call
to crawl past the curtain's seams.
She veers onto the stage, stalled
not, for fear's walled in the wings.

Music of William Byrd

Whether horned, mouthed, or bowed, Byrd
calls forth questing, never null,
not content to extend terse
chords nor disperse pensive pull.

Drawn, ear's forced by searching's sound
onward tow'rds evasive vales
which, though one resolves it round,
are spun to hound with soft sails.

Travel using woven, warm
avenues in hollows heard,
old to us, yet fresh in form
whether horned, mouthed, or bowed: Byrd!

This Mask

How like me this mask I've donned
to bow behind and be seen,
hardened crust of riddled wrongs
whose blustery songs I sing.

Painted over by smug smiles,
what's tainted tugs at its mold.
What it conceals—life's proud prize—
it reveals to eyes grown old.

Know I why in dust I dance
masked and mussed in this fool's flesh,
a quest: course . . . posed by the past,
to grasp which tests the mind's mesh.

What truth would tell is grasped now,
amassed wealth of tooth and task,
my face free to purse its prow
in space—how like me, this mask.

A Briton Reminisces Concerning the Horse

Celts' high view held of the horse
naught else has the force to fill.
It helped strong wills halt the hordes
rogue lords brought to hound these hills.

Mounted mailed Sarmatians rode
round to spots that raids had razed.
Steeds staved-in shields; the tales told
of fields' bold deeds gored and graved.

Graved in ground and grief, those days,
lethal, save for sounds of mounts.
Hoofed renown's crisp murmur made
whiskered brigands turn from towns.

Melt miles, gorse-grinder: you knew
no Celt made you a meal's course.
I endorse as tried and true
Celts' high view held of the horse.

Dream of the Reincarnating Soldier

For one who once walked your wiles,
stalked fulfillment's smiles with suns,
played some with a cherished child
(beguiled), perishes, now numbed.

Might mind wend among the Greeks
of Xenophon, dusk's beach bright
with ships ripe with sails that seek
to leap from trail's harried hike.

Calm, the night. I know we sought
what's right, fought so day might dawn,
to make whose cause heeds the hawk
War choose talk that leads to laws.

Hence I did not die for naught:
my hard days bought reason's rise.
Now, sun's miles have had to halt
for one who once walked your wiles.

Raven of War

Clean earth's heft of brittle bones,
the little left of worth's yield.
Through death's still, what reason roams:
a season's groans fill yon field.

Feast, raven of war: the wind,
craven, has teased its sore scent,
aftermath of a dire din
where ire and wrath, to win, went.

Anger urged victor; the vexed,
nicked or purged, in languor lie.
Right some beak should need them next:
hexed, they feed the chic and shy.

Fly, once skittish, folded frame
emboldened by British blood:
tearing, gorge on men (these maimed
kin), not shamed to ford this flood.

Meat of the skald's skill, oft-sung
feats now fill cold halls with loss,
bites now 'nstead, ruthlessly wrung
where inked heads toothlessly toss.

Nibbling need has brought sky's best:
not your league, those sibling crows!
Raven, whittle lean what's left.
Clean earth's heft of brittle bones.

Warriors in Their Halls at War's End

Red the earth that buoys boasts,
fed by mirth, whose wings are wine.
Dark dreams fade in the tall toasts
as the fall hosts tout each tine.

Horns upturned, war's antlers all
are dulled now, though stern the storms
that made them grow to greet gall
made fleet and small by nixed norms.

Rains wash clean the ravens' roost,
now mere bone: craven their keen.
Swords' work ebbs, while story strews
gory news to set the scene.

High the shields, memory's mirth
when the sky yields gales of ghosts.
Let bards' songs be wed to worth:
red the earth that buoys boasts.

Bovine Excrement

All poets are liars, lost
deep in briars of tall tales.
Figures of speech incur cost:
when glibly tossed, their force fails.

Credibility wanes, worn
down by silly games and gall,
which teach ears that bards are born
forsworn liars each and all.

In Tir na nOg

In Tir na nOg, a land lost
unabandoned gods that guide.
Winter's brisk, and summer soft,
sun aloft over hills' hide.

Youth abides—ideal the day—
while the real world's age grows old.
Touched, thought turns to mist what may
miss today as it burns bold.

There do the gods whose gift spurs
odds' *up*lift outlast our flesh.
Sung of, it can wear our words—
I dare birds to feel this fresh!

Son of Finn will take my tear
and win me one in fear's frost.
Cost? the hand of her I hear
in Tir na nOg, a land lost.

Deibhidhe

This is the only form I know of that Irish and Welsh traditions have in common, though each tradition embellishes it in its own way, the Irish with cross-rhyme and the Welsh (who call it *cywydd deuair hirion*) with *cynghanedd*. I sometimes revert to the earlier Irish requirement, called *rinn*, stipulating simply that the second end-word of each couplet be one more syllable than the first. In the last example below I have tried to unite the two rhymes of each quatrain by making them a bit similar.

The Mire of Modernity

Skills scatter whose pace the past
pampered, their grace bare ballast.
The bard's craft wastes away, wan
like taste's say, gnarled by neon.

Verbal ties have lost their lure—
digitized, caustic culture!
These trends no seal seems to stem,
no dream's weal mends the mayhem.

Language tools become lost lore:
now numbness rules thoughts' uproar.
Alas, memories still stir,
ill at ease as skills scatter.

Myrddin Expostulates on Friendship to a Bard of the Scotti

Friendship fills its cup with joy's
Gentle glut of old alloys.
Comradeship thrills: in wars waged,
Boldness soars where wrongs rampaged.

Faithfulness stills darkened doubt,
Rates a hold on heart's handout.
Comfort's chills will warm our wit.
Storm the sun! enfold friendship.

Strange Visitor From Another Perspective

Your method troubles me, man:
deft, odd, subtle, quite certain
of unsure things, knowing not
pure truth's ring, there's such racket.

How can you think through the din
of *now* to tweak the tailspin
you consume that consumes you,
fun's tune self-pity's purview?

What projects sorrow's terse tear
erects tomorrow's menhir.
Hand on hope's gravelly grave
gropes towards anguish's enclave.

Each has entered body's cage
self-centered—what an outrage.
You knew then (though mem'ry's minced)
'snot you its pen provinced.

Flesh was new . . . yet old was I!
Fresh: great it grew—self's ally!
Yet once taught otherwise, all
bought truth's cover, care's catchall.

You are not flesh! formless one,
but mind, born of truth's talon.
Rise, self-knowledge: press and prod!
College lies: mind's *your* method.

Deft Is the Dragon

Dragon, dimmed is your gaunt glow
that haunts simmering sorrow.
You I talk of some would slay
for blocking hope's new highway.

Old the truths your talons guard,
value that skirts the schoolyard.
Fearful of what's tried and true,
wide most veer from your venue.

Wake, ways of old: breathe forth fire!
Boldly brave man's warped empire.
Fools see in your death new dawn,
view night in your breath's beacon.

Dark, deliver stars, light's lure,
giver of sight its censure.
Why discard ways that have won?
Day's hard, and deft the dragon.

Mystic Love

I'll admit, if I am pressed,
I am more blessed than unblessed
since light of the moon remains
bright in my inner star-lanes.
My deepest love slept within
then awoke, fixed and elfin.
Chaste is its expression now,

yet passionate, not 'highbrow'.
She's serenity to me,
my calm—the moon's re-entry
into my heart—my sundial,
and balm of rare percentile.

Lady of the Lake in Childhood

Dragon's wings of rain and mist
invite affection's tempest.
Horned and hooded face beset
with grin no child could buffet.

With upturned face, her bright chirps
voice amazement in excerpts—
a breathless torch, lively spurts
of sincere, childlike efforts.

Introvert towards humans, spawn
of druids, she's an icon
of light to dragon's sight, one
to lead both into action.

She knows she has much to learn,
for this one's not a wyvern
but a full dragon, earth's worm
of wisdom for the long-term.

An interchange is gone through
in bursts where none might argue,
mystic increment of school
to grace her unplanned schedule.

Futures not yet clearly drawn
will build upon this bygone,
shaped by her elusive call
to shun the worldly mead-hall.

Séadna

This is probably the most lyrical of the Irish quatrain measures. It shows signs of being related to English ballad meter, but the required cross-rhymes make it much richer, as illustrated by mine once I got the hang of utilizing cross-rhymes.

Stonehenge

Now each sturdy stone has faltered
from that tall rim, that whirled wheel.
Strong structure that once held splendor,
its ruptured throng rendered real.

Footprint of a mighty meaning
now not rightly gleaned nor grasped.
Whose the hearts once here in bunches!
What arts in their clutches clasped.

Footsteps of a mighty message,
since of notions' nest a throne.
Lest my speech grow weak and wordy,
seek rest, now, each sturdy stone.

Tools of Craft's Cunning

Cunning craft shows useful yearnings
nest in every ear that hears.
Similar sounds, fast and frequent,
cast words so their sequence sears.

End-rhyme alone? An old sawhorse!
a holed has-been; a cracked crutch.
More is needed to mold meaning
ere ear hear its keening clutch.

Alliteration stands steadfast:
far forebears leaned on its lilt.
And consonance remains manly,
song's enhanced, uncanny quilt.

And all *in*ternal rhyme's timely:
it chimes at us beneath note.
And grammar's graced with dense talents:
traced, they make a balanced boat.

With all aboard, gall's great gunboat
bristles with force, fore and aft.
All awaits *un*silent running's
tall traits of a cunning craft.

An Irish Poet Praises the Cymry

When there were still bards in Britain,
an ageless art filled each hall
sprung from trees that live as letters,
tools wherewith man's fetters fall.

Numbered sounds kept straight the structure,
plucked pure out of nature's grasp,
poets' pleas caring for crucial
keys: let their solutions last.

Proud people and strong, the Cymry,
rekindling clout beaten low
by Rome, which Eire lost to later,
ours thus glossed the greater glow.

All were once of equal brilliance,
ancillary to sun's sob
seeing lore scorned but smiths smiling,
torn by tiffs' beguiling god.

Under kings of cast most warlike,
light of lore was passed down flawed.
Whispers still ring out with eager
clues, while shouts the leaders laud.

Taliesin's tiered bards were courtly
creatures, their barbs feared at feasts.
Two great chiefs were his hymns' hailing—
bards can be bewailing beasts.

Myrddin was his friend, whose fortunes,
unique, counted his court's end
who'd stood fast *three fortnights* fighting
when forced by swords' bite to bend.

Thence were pagans purged, from borders
terse and tense and plagued with war.
'Twixt Scots, Germans, Christ, and Cymry,
who has priced their mem'ry more!

Before them did fabled 'Merlin'
inable force by breath's bound word,
a boy of seven shown sharpest
of those *grown* whom harpist heard.

He prophesied the tall tyrant's
unsav'ry fall from pied pow'r.
Great Emrys, truth owns you aided
rebirth of Rome's faded flow'r.

Through Arthur's hand your skills scattered
ferocious wills' hackneyed hold.
He led armored men well mounted,
rode down them accounted cold.

Warmth flourished the while you whetted
readied might of burnished blade
to carve out peace from rude raiders,
guard what renewed labors laid.

Looking back, this birth of knighthood
stood for right and for worth's way:
to hoard what was left of learning
from theft by discerning day.

Time's mist houses noble nectar,
arouses risk's stalwart stem.
Tongue gives voice to whine, though whiskered,
this choice wine, this whispered "when . . ."

Scent of the Past

Scented prize of thought, you thunder
    under brown eyes, gently wrought.
Borne on wind's caress, you render
    stormlessness, tenderly taught.

Round your distant dance mine wanders,
    endures angst of the mind's mist,
this to keep from taint of taverns
    deep places your caverns kissed.

Sun's returnings bring their blessings'
    ring of younger yearning's bent.
Swelling sense has found me favored,
    spellbound by your savored scent.

Elegy

Youth once gaped as a great rebirth
stirred man's brute to brave love's limb.
I can still hear song's fair flowers
fill the air to bower's brim.

Spryly we spilled our loves' delight!
Night and day, we tilled our times
till laws phased out love with limits—
today's hardly mimics mine.

Music's light now lurks in corners,
pervasive dearth in night's knell.
Still in life's librettos, lyrics'
echoes fulfill spirits' spell.

What the flower child held holy
eludes now, wild sport of spoof.
Memory strives but trails, turning
to wives' tales my yearning youth.

Once-Upright Flower Children Now Lean

So, the song-wrights pale. A plastic
image of themselves they sell.
My, how pollen's flowers' faded
towers, tall an' jaded, jell!

Your glories once displayed splendor's
worth as nascent inner ore,
mined extract—the selfless, savored
kindness man was flavored for.

Rouse from sleep the slumb'ring model's
ultra-meek yet thund'ring throng.
Moments are love's only ova:
doff the gloves and sow the song!

The You Within Me

With me you are: all the babble
      about hardly has a say.
I, my laugh, my tear, your temple
      here beneath your simple sway.

Though I know your dawns lie distant,
      spent night longs to list you close.
With lips' kiss that roused not recent,
      my licks miss their decent dose.

Part of you is in me always,
      bracing limbs you left to lie
empty of their molded meaning,
      lent them: cold they, singing, sigh.

How those winds of why go whistling
      even now through mist and moon,
teaching the sun's lure its limits'
      reach, a cure to dim its doom.

Who needs daylight when soft silver
      lurks aloft by night—dreams' sieve—
and hope's fluorescent wake, wonder,
      coats with shape the one you're with.

Droighneach
(Modern Specs [Óglachas])

This is the form I 'cut my teeth' on, for the simple reason that it was the only form that allowed more than seven or eight syllables a line. This modern version has a kind of seesaw feel when each end-word is rhymed within that couplet's other line.

Why, Son, a Soldier?

'Tis sudden, son: this sentiment to be soldiering?
Shell-cratering battle's tough and troublesome!
Let others come to grips with strife's smoldering,
shouldering war's slips, cruel and cumbersome.

I'm sensing you feel a deep debt's gratitude:
life's latitude you wish deftly to be defending.
But those whose ending you seek are unsubdued.
And some have viewed it was others caused the contending.

What's sobering is to safely circumvent
being one meant for that awful ogre-ing.
Don't grow a sting: don't act to others' detriment.
'Tis sudden, son, this sentiment to be soldiering.

Docile Can Be Dangerous

With any but bland babes, docile can be dangerous:
too many so can change for us the peace possible
through strength to defeat's fossil by a lax, languorous
mood of unreadiness and being bossable.

It also opens the door to dour oppression
from the inside, a lesson learnt heretofore
by the Framers: to restore freedom's gift, aggression
was required, to lessen oversight evermore.

It's a definite plus if all understand
this seemingly grand world can rise up rancorous.
Lest war's impetus find our army undermanned
with any but bland babes, docile can be dangerous.

Hawthorn Blossoms

In scent's subtle edge, in splendor bright and beautiful
on hedge or bush, tenderness is an overlay
disguising hard spikes dire and dutiful
that stand as brutal guardian of the everyday.

Like a light dusting of snow, many miniscule
five-petaled spots of white glow thrust forth, threatening
a return to cold from summer's varied vestibule
of bold hues thrumming with warmth's ribald reckoning.

But fear not: exuded pollen, soft *anti*-snow,
eludes eyes but lifts life aloft to copulate
with bloom, while clipped bouquets, of may, face vertigo
up where maypoles play, whose pace we populate.

Your pale purity blocks the way, prevents invasion.
From sensual to demur your mask, mutable,
while minute spears buttress with might your soft persuasion
in scent's subtle edge, in splendor bright and beautiful.

Soldiers of a Great Nation

With care's canopy, you brave distant pavilions
against minions your proud points make panicky.
In you, humanity rises resilient:
you cotillion with none we've not offered amity.

On this delicious earth, death's dance is serious,
sparked by acts imperious and pernicious.
Great warriors quell the vicious, spank the spurious,
wax curious over every scene that's suspicious.

Intelligence, your purpose makes all meaningful:
a gleaning, full, of threats that reek of relevance.
Our walls, well enhanced by your safe ceiling-full,
congealing, fulfill war's plans with apt elegance.

Be prepared is the panoply of the precocious—
against life's grossness, the wise pit sound sanity.
This planet rebounds from doom through your voiced devotion:
the potion is you as shield, with care's canopy.

Relevant Worm

A creature delivering rotating relevance
to man's a feature I'm well-advanced to portraying
in this lamentable lay, this surly circumstance
I have to entrance man's concepts into conveying.

The meaning, in its sometimes dire destiny,
is known not from fantasy, that careless careening
through stars' sheen out beyond man's orb, but from alchemy,
man's inner circuitry—what many are demeaning.

These days it's called a flight of fancy anyway,
the Worm Ouroboros, which may well seem unsightly
yet insightfully embodies the everyday
way of things when viewed tamely and contritely.

Take man's travail as it is: karma's contrivance
has us alive (and suffering) in times entailing
each one eating his own tale, with kindly connivance
of the high self, its revived vision prevailing.

So to the alchemist's glance, the slowly slithering
quivering worm consumes its own end—elegance
in simplicity! a circular dance of dithering!
a creature delivering rotating relevance.

Droighneach
(Old School)

When I discovered the older version of this measure, I adopted it as a means of making verbal music; hence there are a number of them (my cure for boredom). This older form shows itself especially well suited to satire, hence its name, which means 'Thorny', this referring to both satirical force and difficulty of composition.

Hail and Admonition to the Chief

Ah, so't's another term fer which ya were hankerin'—
a banker in slop! Brother, you need ta urinate!
get that drink outta yer system; duly determine
there's no returnin': yuh've pissed 'em! (Tastes terminate.)

Instead, think about rest; recreation; reticence;
get a sense of 'jet striation'; *end* insincere,
so ya can dance about without purpose impingin'
by intention ta werk us over as engineer.

Limo Driver Knows His Place But Finds It Odd

Duty's deference demonstrates enterprise,
a reference to what temper tries that's surprising
yet needed if this fellow is to fraternize,
be mellow, and not satirize unsound surmising.

Greeks with learning served crude Rome: no deft dissenter
let this enter in between earning and temperance.
For though I be a roaring underground aquifer,
the lot prefer thunder drowned in duty's deference.

Heroic Versus Satiric

Two fundamental modes reward the bard's attention.
One's essential, the other merits mentioning.
One's high and heroic, an exacting exemplar;
one's stoic, to dissemble—a terse tempering.

In Homer, it was Iliad versus Odyssey:
one serious—sad—one comedy—false, facetious.
For Dionysus an odd sort of symmetry
or enmity: crying crisis, versus capricious.

One is upraised, one will undercut:
hero thunderstruck, versus crazed percussion.
One who stirs us ending up overstuffed,
versus ogres' roughness or quaint kerfuffle.

Prior to today's asserting of what circumvents
was higher culture content with its curt convention.
Regard one armed with satire as no mean mendicant:
two fundamental modes reward the bard's attention.

If Rhetoric Could Rule the World

Ah, the butter o' me tongue's pearly putterin'
utterin' unsurly wisdom purringly:
If't's what ye'r after, since I'm no slow, slumberin'
butt o' laughter left wonderin', I'll start stirringly.

Speechwise, nuthin's a nearly sa lyrical
spiritchal ear-stuffin' west *ar* east o' Italy
than an Irish lilt, seldom cynical,
in that stylish, spherical tongue Brits speak brittle-ly.

'Tis fluid an' thurrst-quenchin' under ahr tutelage,
a scruple-less drenchin' utherwise, I'm allegin'.
The way Celts handle English is a sweet synthesis.
(We've a fleeter angle on emphasis assessin'.)

'Tshould nevur be even a little bit lackluster
nor a blockbuster o' spittle, this mind musterin'.
Shahrly ya prafers hearts ta be all a-flutter—
ah, the butter o' me tongue's peahrly putterin'!

Cause Yourself: Let Others Blame Others

We dive dext'rously into the universe;
we doom-immerse; head-first we sin, to die diversely.
Life to most is simply a gift of gossamer:
loss irreplaceable, entry ending inertly.

Vain experience tasted by our entreaty
is not completely wasted if we wake fleetingly.
Still, traps thus erected make us uneasy
as faith's money's ejected for tolls, charged teasingly.

For gods laugh at us, while fellow frolickers
pour wrath at us: all glitters like gold—a liturgy.
The wise of us learn to dance like caged conifers,
tall winners of a prize of ample energy.

It's the best we can expect it, the eventful.
Respect it: don't be rude or resentful ventrally.
Serves not truth nor us to blame it on an ancestress:
the infectious swerves not unless we dive dext'rously.

Envoi (Casbairdne):

> Conifer fir's craftier:
> Curbs spread to lift loftier—
> No soft whining 'what-if-er'
> The oft climbing conifer.

On War

I've studied, of man, his stirring, harassed history
of wars' conduct—a mystery's muddied arena.
Its ruthless path's the sorrowed symphony
and borrowed infamy of the amoeba.

Whence come the stalwarts that stand up to the merciless?
Nursing necessity's what such halyards illustrate.
At such times, flaunted skill at arms isn't illicit,
it being implicit the daunted will dissipate.

The bard bringing us wisdom would inherit
thin merit demeaning brave souls at the parapet.
In such straits, valor vaunted apes the angelic!
and gel it should, to help the haunted and delicate.

Peace as premise makes an honest arbiter.
Menace as harbinger makes peace hollow frippery
of whirling sabers, bloodied carvings of canister—
I've studied, of man, his stirring, harassed history.

The Seventh Sea

A half-natural half-cerebral celebrant
is the cathedral sky's elegant eglantine,
whose pink flowers gallivant over the elephant
earth's caravan powers savored at seventeen.

Adventure beckoned sails with wind's wavering,
unreckoned youth savoring its whisper whirringly.
Poignant, remembered anew (though now unnerving),
to've tendered a buoyant unswerving will worthily.

Age-old endeavoring only sea gods authorize—
waves' trough or rise, severing sight from horizons.
Running storms' ravaging brooked no capped compromise,
no taunting lies' savagery save cunning's connivance.

No neighbors near, mostly, no carnival
yarn, evil ghostly nights, only labor's leavening.
Skill advances, warring with what and whenever
then never 'scoring' till port and its taut tethering.

Gulls with their choice cries could soften sacrilege,
or a dolphin's voice, patronage kind and collegial.
Predictably hard-won ocean's a rich, reveried,
typically leather-kneed life, its soul half cerebral.

Humans

We pest herd: unanimous as of yesterday—
less per day, anonymous, yet voiced verbatim.
We reinforce cycles that separate
and fetter, wait on items that dent duration.

We use logic a little, yet are obdurate:
odd your acquittal of us would suppose purity.
What's tongue-in-cheek should have echoes that are accurate
(cheap librettos capture acclaim with *sham* surety).

We ache for the exotic *and* familiar—
neurotic! a mill yearning turns, pushed and pilloried.
Whether whisperer or shouter, must's the mariner
where inner meets outer, and is amply energied.

We're surf, breakers whose crests dwarf us, seldom sensible,
hence a dull spell well done, our angst ebullient.
We curse capers whose jests warp us, elbows akimbo
till hell grows akin, blowing what age makes indolent.

We gather in groups, each an aider-and-abettor,
a Darth Vader cadet parade—perfect getaway.
We *assume* animus, in this soundly sequestered
wee pest herd, unamimous as of yesterday.

Miscellaneous Irish Forms

. . . measures I never got into enough to produce much by way of presentable work.

Play, O Flute of Spring
[Rionnard]

Aftermath of measure,
mend pleasure's path quaintly.
Let each finger firmly
linger, fretting faintly.

Lift winter's spent spirits,
spark lent by swift swallow.
Steady man's moods: mellow
dry wood's heady hollow.

Spring shifts to bright banter:
bold gift, your light leisure.
Make laughter last: linger,
aftermath of measure.

Toothless on the Outside
[Rionnaird Tri-nard]

Toothless on the outside,
sage of sooth, I wander
this wood, act the augur
her lacked sun makes somber.

Someday soon will forest
reek of doom, of dying,
life destroyed, scents scribing
laments, void of vying.

Eyes caught caged in blinders
don autumn's aged decay.
Man's shouldered care creates
what land's cold traits betray.

But crisp, crackling broadleaves
uplift, an odd anchor:
floor's red tiles task anger
to *cast off* roar's rancor.

Passive, the soiled succumb
to coarse goals, roiled, ruthless.
Rot revels in lewdness
that levels, tooled toothless.

Pandora's Alchemy
[Ae Freslighe]

Lead plumb, passion: comical,
numb to all it'll open.
Heating evokes volatile
vapors where spring has spoken.

Summer's silver gossamer
night comes spilling its splendor.

Dawns then the bold blossomer,
gold again, tense and tender.

Great! till the pied pendulum
tries to take it all away.
That's why minds grow minimum,
slowing to time's lie allay.

Human dumbness-deterrence
must tune out fun and fashion.
Can mind's ebb crush recurrence
of time's great lead plumb, passion? [*]

A Fifth Century 'Mistake'

Gaelic Scotti walloping
benign Britons' coasts captured
peach-faced Patrick, galloping
off with 'im, to be 'raptured'.

Where a war would discreetly
have done dent to their dentures,
this thugly thing completely
hog-hobbled the whole venture:

crass crosses' cairns replacing
sacred fires' flames that daily
aired over Eire's embracing
gods of whose make *came* Gaelic!

---

[*] John O'Donovan's *A grammar of the Irish language* refers to this form thus: "There is another species of *Óglachas* [servile meter] which has the first line of each quatrain like *Casbhairn*, and the second like *Rannaigheacht bheag*."

Manger Scene
[Sneadhbairdne]

Darling dioramas children
rush to arrange—
with babe, shepherd, magi, manger,
angel—estrange

sight from Scripture: wise men, faithful,
followed fêted
star, strove long getting there, bedded,
headed ahead,

westward—wearied—to meet Iesus,
safe in *household*,
not babe but *child*. When they boldly
told old ribald

Harod, the land's lord, their story,
his rude response
was to decree death—that monster—
on chance infants

as were under *two*. So *falsehood*
hovers, helping
misshape memory to mingle
ding with darling.

Age's Edge
[Casbairdne]

Age's edge, dregs detected,
aids course where tread's untested.
Still, with its call clandestine,
some fall, with catch requested.

Experience suspended,
fear leaves past tense untempted.

With old wrath's ties untended,
the wise path lies preempted.

Strife's essence gets invested
in stress, life's jest rejected.
Ledge that's safe, sage, ancestral?
age's edge, dregs detected.

"They just wouldn't stay still!"
[*Casbairdne (old school)*]

Mortimer the mortician,
Bored, became a beautician.
Soon, scared by his scrutiny,
Dared many to mutiny.

Where others might mollify,
He didn't quite qualify.
Hence he served them certainer:
Murdered them did Mortimer.

The Cosmos
[*Cro Cumaisc Etir Casbairnde Ocus Lethrannaigecht*][*]

The whole enterprise
open to man's mental probe
tends to temporize:
it speaks only karma's code.

Hence great distances
deceive, for all wends as one,
each dawn's diff'rences
adding to what's same, new-spun.

---

[*] My source is Poetry Magnum Opus (Tinker) online; elsewhere, with the spelling *Casbairdni*, it has syllable count 7-5-7-5.

The plump period
it takes heaven's whole to whirl[*]
mounts up myriads,
the sun's cycle in the world.

Grant *some* sympathy
for old ways that saw man's soul
etched in infamy
and yoked yearly to the whole.

To a Soldier

[*Lethrannaegecht Mor*]

Hail, warrior, well met:
far a fellow that!
Brave, lingers in light—
one bright core of cat!

It's lucky for us
we lack not such souls
amongst our number
to stir when wrath rolls.

Were we all peaceniks,
where's war's wherewithal?
We'd soon be but slaves
or graves—you're our wall!

Best for the whole world
you haul ass war-wise.
You're out for them too,
see life through their eyes.

You're *made* of the world's
muddy boots, you bet!
Therefore all the more:
hail warrior, well met!

---

[*] (precession of equinoxes, in which the heavens revolve in a forward sense around the *zodiac*)

Evils Merlin Felled

Much mischief attempts
to touch Merlin's myth—
as if yell of youth
tossed truth off a cliff!

Artorius, teen
leader, learnt from him
valor, and prevailed
with mailed might of limb.

Britons' sky was scorched
by sly heathens' hands,
by grim brigand's boot
seeking loot and lands.

Amerlinus made
fate turn back to bright
from dark shadows shorn
of morn's looming light.

Tears for the dead doused
fear's blackening flame
because heroes held,
spelled by knack and fame.

Hail! Merlin, manly
blackbird; prince of peace
in war's well. You led,
while sheep fled their fleece.

Ear heard Jutes go "bah"
fearing your firm clutch.
We of good faith find
we owe your mind much!

What To Do After Using This Stanza Form
[*Deibhidhe Baise Fri Toin*]

Bend, slowly,
like a roused roly poly:
curl back up into a small
ball.

Just maybe
the dumb-idea navy
then won't find you where you wend.
Bend!

Celtic-Themed Poems
in
Other Poetry Forms

*These are to disabuse dear reader of any notion that I, like most of my
contemporaries, am unable to compose in good English meter. Phooey!*

The Sun-Hero

Born is the hero, cradled by the *birch*,
then taught, sheltered by gentle *rowan*'s boughs;
he grasps the oar whose handle is of *ash*,
becomes a bridge with *alder* for its pilings,
and weaves the *willow* withies of his fate,
now separated off by *hawthorn*'s hedge

~ dead and reborn beneath the sky's broad *oak* ~

which *holly* then surrounds, whose crowd of points
finds wisdom in the nutshell *hazel* makes
to spread along a *vine* to the divine
child now crowned with *ivy*—Dionysus—
whose *whitten*-berry ink plays through his reed
as guardian *elder* guarantees sweet rest.

The pulsing of the willows in the winter wind

So far away from my ancient tribe of Gaelic heroes,
Far from the ancient harp's immortal, warming cry,
Far from the battles of the hardened, fearsome warriors
Who fought by rigid forms and did not fear to die.

We squat on nature's back and shun its bosom's warmth.
The womb of earth brings forth her fruit in angry sobs.
Squeezed dry of purpose, now instead of forest songs
Our lives' concerns are forests of keys, switches, and knobs.

S, Saille, Willow, Spring's Fount

Willow, your wellspring of emotions pour
in torrents from the fount of spring you are,
long seen a symbol of deep winter's war
lamented once the blooms of spring appear
on forest floor whose bursts of color mar
cold winter's former tapestry of fear.

Why Willows Weep

appearance says
they are forlorn
their boughs drooping
as if to mourn
yet poets know
why willows weep
it's just one more
secret they keep
they imitate
the fount of spring
and overflow
with burgeoning

Hymn in Praise of Luck (Lugh the Many-Skilled)

Though it were just this single tongue
    that bend to sing his praises,
his ample skills, forever young,
    could not help but amaze us.

When asked his craft, the crafts he had
    were listed for the sentry.
'Twas numberless they were, full glad
    the gods to grant him entry.

A harper, bard, and farrier,
    a carpenter, a tanner,
a healer, smith, and war-ri-or—
    a hero by his manner.

The list went on and on for him,
    and though each task was manned,
no god but him had all of them
    in all of that green land.

For Luck in all things doth excel,
    in chess, in war, in song,
and still today when all goes well
    is when he tags along.

Anubis Annwfn

Anubis, old when dynasties were young,
your mysteries once reached beyond the land
where pyramids spear skies, to which were sung
the spells that made us poets by your hand.
On Britain's plains, the Otherworld was named
Annwfn, by which I sense your presence there
when bards made song and chiefs would listen, shamed
or lauded by the lines that spilt their air.

The dead have seen the gate to power's source,
whose guardians shamans trick who aim to steal
the secrets that endow with greater force
to overcome the hurt our lives reveal.
To guard the dead from the wild jackals jaws
opens the way to fortune's deeper cause.

Merlinus Ambrosius (Ambrosius Avrelianus)

When Rome departed, while the Britons feared
Irish and Saxon brigands seeking plunder,
a well-born Roman leader, much revered,
insured civility would not go under.
A prodigy, while yet a child he solved
great engineering riddles and foretold
the Britons' fate—what soon he'd be involved
in making come to pass, by acting bold.
Sarmatian horse, whose veterans once served
the Roman Wall, with foresight he embraced,
whose fish-scale armor and long lance unnerved
those bands of heathen helms on foot they faced.
'Twas thus he set the stage for brave Artorius
to triumph with these 'knights' in battles glorious.

Battle and Aftermath
[*Three 'Princess' Sonnets*]*

Pounding of hooves where skirted steel would flail
sailed wildly through as Saxons swarmed around
failing to form back up amidst the sound
hounding one's ears, while some, shunning to bail,
found flesh with spear—yes, even through that mail
hailed unsurpassed protection, made of bound
trailed (overlapped) iron plates—till some were downed,

---

* i.e. with inverted rhyme scheme in first syllables

gowned now in courage in the poets' tale.
When carnage cooled, each strong Sarmatian 'knight'
right then would pause, relax just where he'd been,
twenty-span lance laid down. The evening's bite,
blighted by mostly Saxon dead again,
sent darkness to restore the peace till light,
bright-spread by morning, brought to eyes war's din.

While squires and women healers went about
outguessing death (when lucky), fortune's smile
filed proudly over faces from the shout
routed to be picked up across a mile.
Artorius raised up his bow, the vile
bile at last subsiding as the jar
marring his thirst found lips—to reconcile
style with the reinstatement of his star.
Bright red had peril been: it placed the bar
far nearer than the past to that dark height
might might have failed to leap did Luck not spar
partisan for him to restore the right.
Naught threatened now to block the outcome sought,
bought dearly by these men with whom he'd fought.

Calmly, that afternoon, lieutenants sat
at council with their leader whilst a psalm,
balm of the faithful, sounded, then a fat
vat of strong drink filled horn in each stout palm.
Craftily now, the captured Saxon earl,
surly and maimed, was dragged out: bloodied aft
(shaft having been extracted), he would whirl
burly with blows on anyone who laughed.
At last they saw their Duke, with great ado,
mew the old hawk himself! then push the slats
that latched his cage as they all watched him stew—
new-buoyed were they to have caged the rat.
"Here, here!" they shouted and with a hearty cheer
tearfully hailed the fruit of one tough year.

And Untoward the Dust

With the hoofbeat of horse and untoward the dust
they have clashed on the grass, with the footsoldier's thrust
counterbalanced by weight of momentum and 'mussed'.

And the steeds that had proved unremittingly swift
in arriving at strife offered 'knighthood' a lift
both in height and sheer push in event he be miffed.

Having spotted the foe by the trail of demise
he had left in his wake, they'd the gift of surprise
as they prodded their mounts with the grip of their thighs.

And the reavers beheld their destruction descend
on their heads and deal wounds that their yells would not mend,
sending souls to a place where the spoils cannot spend.

They were Frisian rogues of the sea-raiding type
who were caught on dry land ere their ships were in sight,
and they fell to a man, falling prey to dislike.

There's a dust that is raised even now on that moor:
muffled yells of the rovers are battle's stale spoor
as they wander the dark seeking pillage, their lure.

[Epilogue:]   Is it wrong to associate anapests' beat
             with the galloping hooves of the horse?
Come the snow or come hail or come rain or come sleet,
             humble servant, it steadies the course.

Bardic Attitude
[*Hexameter Triolet*]

How should the eyes that read this say I honored them
in posing it: by content? or by turn of phrase?
If some such humble work of mine were classed a gem,
how should the eyes that read this say I honored *them*

and not this flesh, of which I'm president pro tem?
Indeed if *all* my writings managed to amaze,
how should the eyes that read this say I honored them?
In posing it! (by content *or* by turn of phrase).

The Wild Man, the Sea-Fortress

quaint old apple tree
'shelter of a hind'
the Irish poets call you
but me I see you as sweet fruit or an old friend

in moments when I'm lucid which is mostly
you seem the center of my world
is it become that small or am I
simply short of physical sight to see that far

there have been storms that have beaten and battered
here near the world's source this primeval wood
but then when I stood
near you underneath your boughs I felt them not

what do King Wreathe-Rick's hunters have on me
that I cannot undo
by clinging to you and whispering the name
we knew you by when last I was here on earth

they call *me* Myrddin
        the 'Sea-Fortress'
but they don't even guess your name (it's safe with me)
womb of the world of fruitfulness
and refuge from barbs

quip me a question asker of end results
I'll try to answer it without notice
of the *quirk* made by your letter
        Q whew
sound of a bite being taken out of you

but you know that and speak the sound willingly
by offering sweet solace
       to hunger
       and thirst
to the hunted hind
       fleeing monkish arrows

you remember Piglet
hunters got him when I was elsewhere
o would he were here to talk to
he would at least talk back

you'll do as friends go
you offer comfort even by your silence
neat trick if a man did it
or even a woman

when you were young I was young
seeking a womb's softness from the outside
you busied yourself making your quick quake
of sweetness available to our advances

I envy you your constant giving
even now you give me calm memories
of when I was sane at all times
before *awen* took me

Vision-Walking on the Scottish Borders
[sonnet using line-end consonant-repetition in place of rhyme]

The schemes upon these hills are voiced, in passing,
to no-one, really, yet to me—offset
and linked only by dreams—sing freedom's lapsing,
the steely individual now fenced.
Approaching horsemen, ghosts of time—yet threat
no less to knowledge of what passed *before*
these coarse men of the cross got round its throat—
outnumber Love: a battle lurks—ebb, fear!

If Gwenddolau be gone, so much the more
does Mere-Then's wailing song surmount these trees
(his shelter's spawn): ask eyes what turned them wry
and you will hear him flailing in his tears.
For he saw freedom's death back then as well,
in breath of men on both sides of the Wall.

Out of Kindness, Joy: A Moment in the Life of Dreon the Brave[*]

Bellowing warrior he, proud veteran
Of many fights with towering, muscled slayers
From other, stranger outlooks than the one
He championed against Rome's vain surveyors.
A pagan to his death, he would not bow
Before some god who thought himself alone
Even in forests which old gods endow
With holiness firm majesty has shown.
Yet when confronted by one meagre child
Who stepped in front of him to save her house
From being pillaged, he, no longer wild,
Softened like Aesop's lion to the mouse
That gnawed the net through for him as he bent
To comfort her from tears, his fury spent.

Sound-Understanding

How potent are the sounds of human speech:
the hissing Sss of serpents; the forceful slap,
sharp T-,[†] of waves against the sides of ships;
the thud of Thunder's hammer, D-; the first
attempts at sound in babies, B-; or Nnn,
the wind that plays the rigging's harp-strings; H-,
the breath that fragrant flowers evoke; or Qu-
or Hw-, the sound of biting into apples.

---

[*] nephew of Gwenddoleu
[†] letter followed by hyphen means make the *sound* of that letter

My favorite is the moan that savors grapes
or other sweetnesses, self-contained Mmm.
Then there's the punch of the gut-wrenching G-.
And K-, that other sound close-in astride
the gullet, signifying what's held close.
And then there's P, epitome of speech.
How wise those ancient Kabbalists and bards,
who symbolized with trees these sounds' effects:
the *oak* of Zeus as D; the writhing *willow*
as S; the sharp slap of the waves as T,
the *holly*; a child's B the *birch*, whose size
is often small compared to other trees
and whose white bark presages innocence;
the sea-wind, N, as *ash*, the wood of oars;
and fragrant H as *hawthorn*; and the Q
of apples as the *apple*; and the Mmm
of savored sweetness as the *vine* of wine's
origin; G, the sound that grabs the gut,
as clinging *ivy*; K, which signifies
that which is gathered close, as *hazel*, tree
from which diviners cut divining rods
and summers' nuts (and fruits), now gathered close;
and holy P, that sound that signals speech
itself, as *whitten*, from whose berries ink
is made. I laud the poet-priests of old—
those druids, and those prophets of the Jews—
who formulated a sound-understanding
embodied in the symbols which became
the letters of the alphabet, to tame
the wild currents of speech in such a manner
that keeps what's sweet distinct from Thunder's hammer.

'Heathen' Lament

Vast schemes the hills in passing speak
to no-one, really, yet to ears
like mine, who dream the distant years,
sing freedom's lapse in every squeak,

each brittle bending branch too meek
to stop the horseman that appears—
a ghost through mists—as ghost-steed rears
announcing battle's echoed peak.
His chieftain rests; but Myrddin sings,
hoarsely decries death's cross that swept
through hills where once fierce gods stood guard.
That oak-imprisoned poet clings
to freedom, while the limbs he's leapt
salute with leaves their ancient bard.

Mistletoe Moon

Orb only partly veiled by the ice crystals flying
high in the frigid night's exalted spaces,
what do you bring me but the fruits of my own emptiness
gathered with love for the instruction of the upstart in me.
I crave your wisdom beyond that of sun and stars,
for you are closer. Did not your recent crescent birth
occur when the year was dying and the harper strummed
to have some words with supper? It was not out of *need*
(that rune of handles and tool shafts made
of ash that stands at the world's hub)
     that you appeared
but from the bosomed womb of the last gasp of decaying
day, when the shade of elder fell across our path
and allowed this cycle's ride into the sunset:
     it was then that you appeared,
so that you might direct the year's rebirth.

The sun is following *your* ups and downs
     only slower
however much it believes itself the center
     and time at its command.

Song of Samhain

The moist willow of spring has poured
      its plenty over *awen's* ear
whose corn has flourished and now is stored
      for winter's want with Samhain near.

Prepare a place the honored dead
      may join us in our harvest fling;
no seance tricks shall mar what's said
      by those who can no longer sing.

For on the morrow, winter wends
      across the threshold of the day,
so we salute the hour that sends
      the sun its otherworldly way.

The Wales of My Heart
[*'Welsh' sonnet (7-syllable lines rhymed ababccb dedeffe)*]

Dear sweet land I have not seen
as yet in my wanderings,
land of poets' deep-felt sheen
of light kindled insight brings
from mines deep inside the earth
of soul's substance, given birth
in bless'd lands where genius sings.
Druids' knowledge of the skies
within our hearts was once taught
to bards living where the wise
were free to spout all they thought
worthy: though the Romans slew
most of them, the things they knew
whisper to us still when sought.

APPENDIX:
Moral and Metaphysical Themes

It is a poet's duty to expound deeper truths, to act as druid if qualified, and I count myself lucky to have answered most outstanding questions puzzling philosophers. I call myself *idiot savant* and feel I share that status with the late Stephen Hawking (facile at math, idiot at cosmology). I *get* metaphysics, and ancient mysteries, can correct modern physics, have learned stars are electric discharges; yet at making a living, I am clueless. In the following several items, *con*tent trumps poetics, thus *somewhat* betraying my expressed taboo against prose-poetry: a joking Rhupunt; three in dark age Briton style; eleven *cyhydedd naw ban*; four that use Irish forms.

You Poets Need To Tone Down Those Metaphors

'Bout all they teach figures-of-speech-wise in high schools
is metaphor, simile, or (most clear to fools)
imitating nature using phonetic tools,
called onomatopoeia: what . . . *bubbles* in pools

Now those last two are fine and do enhance words' feast.
But that first bit, metaphor, it—which I like least—
sometimes projects the ill-effects of a fanged beast.

Once some sage said, "My beast is dead," humans began
to sacrifice them and entice gods' hunger, man
practicing this through an abyss of time's broad span.

Some bard who'd reached a high state preached we should snuff out
our humanness—what made this mess! This led, no doubt,
the ruling scum to get blood from a human spout.

Thence, altars bore humanoid gore—high maintenance!
Then some poor priest whose wits increased through abstinence
told men: "Give up lust's meager cup for sustenance!"

So misplaced zeal rose to appeal to the Goddess
where youths, once good, 'trimmed' their manhood in their madness.
Well-meant or not, metaphor's got lots to confess.

Grappling with Themes

   Struggled hard
   over how to best
   present the past.
History's tale has managed well as a peltast
   able to fell
   Goliath
   with lessons cast.
Why would you accept my tale if any less?

   Tongue, draw forth
   heroes' breaths:
   convey largesse.
Be shape's shifter where fate's sifter is feckless.
   Who won fame
   in what grand game
   the gods embraced?
Who's stood forth as north in the tough tests we've faced?
   we humans of all stripes
   who are worth
   not waste . . .

Offer air
impressions blessings'
spells make last
thus to fashion verse as wisdom's terse repast
in this valley
of the venturesome
and the vast.

Eve (חוּה)

inscribed emptiness? blank page? her
whose name meant 'life'? I aver
she came not from some lean larder
of *male*ness in that world-spawning stir

two is always everywhere preceded by *one*
hence sexless Adam Qadmon sprang she from
which juncture caused
       it-ness to be flung
off-center
       to where it has become
male
the stronger
       according to some

not perceiving in fact that two were yet one
is what has spun immortality's curfew
in whose night we humans drift askew

look at man
       obviously
a two-columned form
       one column clearly
broken off
       so that the womb might be

taking 'rib' for *side*
       the side towards sight

'fruit' for womb
> scene of gestation's might
and scripture for poetry
> what insight
remains that would question
> Eve's Light?

metaphysical shorthand for truth
versus a failed theory's blind reproof
for which the fossil record builds no roof
what was predicted was gradual
and the change found
> sudden
> sweeping
> full
refutation by nature of man's bull

not perceiving in fact that the two were one
is what has spun immortality's curfew
and in that night humans still drift askew

The Great Fallacy

Think you there's one self we all share, not many?
This is what I call the Great Fallacy.

Did not the Buddha help us see
one shouldn't accept what doesn't agree
with reason and common sense? How could it be
that individuals accrue karmic debris
whose weight is not their own but actually
belongs to some single Self that we,
who all must suffer, share? This perplexity,
a misconstruing of the central Unity,
misleads myriads of monks who flee
the very thing that offers them the key:
acceptance of self-responsibility.

I entreat ye, seekers of the Way, to cease
trying to weasel out of the ancient lease
you signed when you no longer were at peace:
disharmony *you made* is now your fleece.

Wear it and it will do its bit to teach
the path open to all who would impeach
sensation's rule over the psyche's reach.

Other Worlds (Shaman's Song)

Renewed intermediary I
between worlds: the world of the sky
and its beings; this one; and realms that lie
deep in the earth, to which shamans fly
through ducts and openings on the sly.

I can describe the vast palace grounds
of the celestial beings and their hounds
that heap riches onto terraced mounds—
worship as the source of what abounds,
and yes, that was meant the way it sounds.

In the earth's interior is where
to seek spirit allies if you dare,
animal spirits with whom we share
interests and the world—au confrere—
and retrieve lost souls hungry for air,
their bodies ill since they wandered there.

I'm a traveler above, below,
and sideways, humankind my cargo.

Gnostic Alchemist's View

All life is filth. Human life, of course.
Animal life, despite dog and horse.
Vegetable life, filth's very source
save for those few venerated trees
that named letter-sounds' identities
in the old druid academies.
Mineral life, too: the end effect
of filth—dead filth, best one can expect
until the mind is poised to reject
all life as filth in its current form
and take the eternal as the norm,
flesh that overpowers passions' storm.

Life—in both inception and decline—
is filth; a never-depleted mine
of filth; an ever-depleted line
of renewal of filth in due time
attempting to refine life's mere grime
to rival filth in its very prime!

Cleanliness must mark the distant goal:
a self cleansed of the rest of the whole,
axis pointing back, towards life's high knoll,
responsibility's high threshold
(and the future's only firm foothold).

The Age of Men

At some point on this stalled arc of decline
you'll pine to have men back, the hallmark
of a stable folk, back from the dark
pit you've pinned them in with your black mark.

Your vilifying has made him less
than he'd normally be in this mess.

Peace through strength: the only way that works.
Where's the strength in a world full of perks?

What you know of World War One is false:
it started because men learned to waltz.

Oneness not championed by bold hearts
leaves folks bickering by fits and starts.

How to Tell the Blowhards (How to Tell Them What?)

To see the world in caricature
is just a joke till you have tenure,
at which point you menace youths' impure
        minds.
Moon days!
        Are you willing to immure
your kid in boxed-up thinking?
        Endure
that and it's like a clear aperture
next to real political stature
given over entirely to your
dreamer of cartoon dreams,
        who is sure
they're real because he's made them so,
        cure
that he is to all that's ill.
        Inure
us all from such tyrants:
        they posture
who have not the goods,
        only allure.

The Twin Towers After These Dozen Years

Sinews of commerce, ripped from mercy
by death's sour delight, what unsightly
imprint on memory our eyes see
in your torn moment. Mourn with me old wrongs
and intone song's ode on the sandy
wave-worn cheeks woe's calm seeks in your lee,
when winds of turmoil roil in mighty
swirls of hatred's smoke. How tired are we
of rancorous flame, of incessant blame—
       a recurrent shame, and still shoddy!

Neither age nor spent rage has erased
that day's daze nor night of blight we faced
fearing further crimes, whose fervent haste
warriors' worth despoiled that spilled a taste
of turnabout on terrain abased
by hate's slaves in dim-lit caves encased.

My tongue's tint feels its stint at tribute
fall short as ire fills its ashen root,
whose fallen tree, downed, has faltered, mute
and eloquent as night's quiet lute
in undimmed witness, limned to refute
cartoon causes slaughterers impute
to those they burned for being astute.

Alchemy's Elements

After centuries claiming the four
were superstition, physics did more:
it proved them! and thus opened a sore
on science's skin—quick, close the door!
(so no-one finds out). Better to bore
by lack of progress than to restore
what we had discredited before.

But I was not misled in the end
and stumbled on the truth, which won't bend
to please priests of the Quark, who would spend
billions for colliders that won't mend
the main flaw in their plan: can't suspend
nature's innate laws. They have weakened
empiricism's reign, whilst they tend
their enclosed particle garden's blend
of truth and lies. The non-reverend
run the sciences now, their stipend
fat to hide how far from truth they wend.

Knowledge Waves at the Roiled Threshold of a Dark Age

when life quickens
  I anticipate
wave upon wave
  let through the floodgate
on infertile land
  to irrigate
the fertile patches
  rather than wait
for earth
  which I do concede is great
to on its own repopulate
  restock
the block
  new neighbors for the ingrate
fishes and such
  that survive each quake
in the foundation
  when mountain's shake
the cold off
  enriched by the mandate

Knowledge Waves 2

No equation originated
us, nor some obtuse 'God'. In their stead
man has eternally existed,
patterned on the divine. Once misled
by math's abstraction, minds forfeited
sound science in trade for power's head—
conservation laws violated,
basis of all physics uprooted
by algebraic tricks. We are fed
droppings of Taurus and put to bed.

Meanwhile, the monotheistic Gods
must have been ministered to by clods:
eternal Creator—of synods!—
yet He only started crafting sods
a short time ago? What are the odds!

Isaac Asimov was indignant
creationists be thought relevant
yet adhered to a crazed covenant
whose absurdity's just as poignant.

Knowledge Waves 3

The universe has always been. Proof:
the existence of eternal truth.
The structure of number is a thing
on which time's flux can have no bearing.
Non-warped minds can see that geometry
     has this quality too to its sting,
Riemann and Einstein notwithstanding.
Four elements subdivide nature,
have tenure over time's hollow ring;
moreover the roots of their being
arise from geometry's having
points and lines, angles and solid things.

Knowing such truths gives one's sandals wings!
To comprehend these vast reckonings,
we must be eternal too: the means
of recognizing lack of endings.
There must always *be* upright beings—
sentient Anthropos—whose mind's schemes
have shaped the world we know. And it rings
true the more distant the past, the less
relic remains of it through the stress
and excavations of the countless
civilizations passed, whose access
predated ours. Plus the evidence
found is filtered through academe's fence.
But some crept through before it got tense.
Pre-Jurassic strata gives us hints:
smooth metal spheres make an appearance.
And the gap is really quite immense
between fossils' trace and Darwin's 'sense'.

Yes, we were a higher creature once,
next whom today's human's a mere dunce.

And Its Dance

insubstantial gains
      squander merit
the problem
      is sanity's exit
debt upon debt
      while bigwigs fidget

revolution's due
we need to spit
      out
the current clout
bring sense
      into it

unfortunately revolutions
use-you-ly fall short of solutions
it's the way fate repays insouciance

karma's a beach
      head-in-the-sand stance
can't miss
the tidal wave
      and its dance

acute armageddon lurks

when the memory is a reverse
      sieve
soothed with or without
      room to be terse
no wonder
we're governed
      for the worse

acute armageddon lurks
      in the blood
on though blade go
      still a bulldog irks
if you ask me
the world's run
      by jerks

Man Progresses Both Forward and Backward
[*Rannaigheacht Mhor*]

On man plods, to head, to hind,
to hide, bled, in the soft sod,
gone the way what posed as pride
is spied now, through clay and clod.

Bright costumes adorn each dawn,
garb donned when the norm is new,
the bright fling of summer's song
gone that rung once trite but true.

Ages up and down are led.
The fashions found all ebb, timed
by fate's whims, which odds don't wed.
On man plods, to head, to hind . . .

Law's Purpose: To Limit the Cult of the State
[*Droighneach (old school)*]

Limiting size, scope, and power granted government
underwent mimicking before finely fermented
into lip-service alone, that half abhorrent
torrent that rings a bit nervous, its truth tormented.

A real problem looms here: can we cauterize
the wound? authorize sanity's solemn arising?
Powers lacking the smarts to ruefully recognize
the true bully jeopardize commerce with conniving.

I'm but an aging eighteenth-century liberal
whose raging vigor'll fail freedom thoroughly
unless you're swayed by my words and turn from temporal
fads to confess the truth, commensurate morally.

Be wise: *on* to the wiles of the savvy sultanate's
horizon-grabbing gulp in its fit of annexing
what it can't produce itself. It's the ultimate
cult 'n' it fears we'll reduce it with law's limiting.

After Plato

Certainty of opinion, the mad mandolin
of lectures, grand omen of dust's dominion:
where's your belated sting, o daft daffodil
that cremated math-mobile airs in curt cotillion?

All that's *ever* known are matters eternal,
wee kernel *within* the tatters of time's tournaments.
Things worldly can change: doubts determine
that they return unearned regard with *play* permanence.

Let mind wax empirical, to enrapture
then capture the meant miracle: being *accurate.*
To be too sure means dancing with disaster,
this after enhancing things angry and aspirate.

A special risk is the unanswered and internal:
infernal or celestial, it will throb thermally
till some self-unctuous air opt to uncurtain
some burden half seen . . . but in sumptuous certainty.

Today's 'Natural Philosophers'
[*Deibhidhe*]

Christ, the perfected man, sees
our world centered in bodies
that house sentience and Light,
beings whose stance is upright:
sees a universe centered
where nature's weight and the Word
meet and interact, where thought
must face the senses' onslaught.

Servants of the senses claim
man is only an endgame
begun in chaos—physics
parading as creatrix,

human beings a mere quirk
of evolution's network,
apes that dropped down from the trees
as gentlemen and ladies.

Don't *credit* philosophers
and scientists, cadavers
of a dead world who exalt
Chance, and rockets, and asphalt.
Adhere to what can be known,
not theories, not the cyclone
of disordered minds claiming
more thunder than they can sing.

FIN